John Cunningham Clyde

Rosbrugh

A tale of the revolution

John Cunningham Clyde

Rosbrugh
A tale of the revolution

ISBN/EAN: 9783337343873

Printed in Europe, USA, Canada, Australia, Japan

Cover: Foto ©ninafisch / pixelio.de

More available books at **www.hansebooks.com**

ROSBRUGH,

A
TALE OF THE REVOLUTION,

OR

LIFE, LABORS AND DEATH

OF

REV. JOHN ROSBRUGH,

Pastor of Greenwich, Oxford and Mansfield Woodhouse (Washington) Presbyterian churches, N. J., from 1764 to 1769; and of Allen Township church, Pa., from 1769 to 1777;

CHAPLAIN IN THE CONTINENTAL ARMY;

CLERICAL MARTYR OF THE REVOLUTION,

Killed by Hessians, in the battle of Assunpink, at Trenton, New Jersey, Jan. 2d, 1777.

Founded upon a paper read before the New Jersey Historical Society at its meeting in Trenton, January 15th, 1880; to which is appended genealogical data of all the Rosbrughs of the connection in America;

BY

REV. JOHN C. CLYDE, A. M.,

Author of "History of Allen Township Presbyterian Church"—of which Mr. Rosbrugh was pastor when killed—and of "Genealogies, Necrology and Reminiscences of the Irish Settlement, Northampton county, Pennsylvania"—where Mr. Rosbrugh recruited his company.

EASTON.
1880

Entered according to act of Congress, in the year 1880, by
JOHN C. CLYDE,
In the Office of the Librarian of Congress, at Washington.

Fac-simile of autograph, enlarged in the proportion of 1 *to* 2, *made in the Allen Township Church book, November* 22d, 1774.

PREFACE.

This TALE OF THE REVOLUTION, or historical sketch of one who figured in, and lost his life amid the scenes connected with that ever memorable struggle, has the following history, viz.: The author was invited to make an address, in August, 1879, at the Harvest-home of the Greenwich Presbyterian church, in Warren county, New Jersey. The spot designated for the festivities was upon the banks of the Pohatcong creek, one-half or three-fourths of a mile from the site of the original Greenwich church, in which Rev. John Rosbrugh was ordained to the christian ministry.

The author thought it might be appropriate and interesting to speak of the beginnings of things among the people in whose festivities he had been invited to participate. He accordingly spoke of their first pastor, Rev. John Rosbrugh.

A request was made the same day for a copy of the manuscript that the address might be published. As it had been entirely of an extemporaneous character, this request could not be complied with. The public press however, took up and published an outline of the remarks made, by which means it came to the attention of an officer of the New Jersey Historical Society. A request was preferred by him that the subject-matter of the address be put into a suitable form for reading before the Historical Society. Accordingly the author prepared the address and read it before the Society, at its meeting in Trenton, Jan. 15th, 1880.

As the author subsequently received a number of applications for copies of the address, he decided to put the same in print, and therefore the following pages, founded upon the paper read before the Historical Society, are in the hands of the reader.

The address as presented here, has been divided into short chapters for the convenience of the reader; and at the head of each page is given a brief statement of the main subject-matter of that page. All the facts are preserved which were presented to the Historical Society, and in addition, many things in greater detail than time and circumstances then would justify the author in entering upon.

The final chapter has been added in order that the whole of the Rosbrugh connection in America might in this brief manner be linked together; and this was thought to be a suitable ending, since the two brothers who came across the sea are brought forward together in the opening of the address.

As additional information was continually coming to hand whilst the work was going through the press, on a number of points explicit statements will be found in the latter pages, which were passed over as uncertain or unknown, in the early part.

The sources from which the author has drawn information, outside of his own personal researches, are duly recognized from time to time as they appear, in the body of the work.

BLOOMSBURY, N. J., JUNE, 1880.   J. C. C.

CONTENTS.

FAC-SIMILE of autograph, enlarged in the proportion of 1 to 2, made in the Allen Township Church book, November 22d, 1774.

MAP to illustrate early history of Rosbrughs in America.

MAP to illustrate the position of the American and British armies previous to the battle of Trenton, Dec. 26th. 1776—at which the Hessians were captured—and the battle of Assunpink, or second battle of Trenton, Jan. 2d, 1777—at which Mr. Rosbrugh was killed.

MAP to illustrate the march of the American army after the battle of Princeton, to the winter-quarters at Morristown, in 1777, which closed the campaign in which Mr. Rosbrugh's company participated.

DIAGRAM to illustrate the battle of Trenton, Dec. 26th, 1776—at which the Hessians were captured—and the battle of Assunpink, or second battle of Trenton, Jan. 2d, 1777—at which Mr. Rosbrugh was killed.

DIAGRAM to illustrate the battle of Princeton, where Mr. Rosbrugh's company fought, Jan. 3d, 1777.

PREFACE.

PAGE.

CHAPTER 1.
EARLY LIFE.
Name.   Nativity.   Education.   1

CHAPTER II.
PREPARATION FOR THE MINISTRY.
A beneficiary.   Licensure.   4

CHAPTER III.
FIELD OF LABOR IN NEW JERSEY.
Preaching points. Old Greenwich. Mansfield Woodhouse. Oxford.   8

CHAPTER IV.
MINISTRY IN NEW JERSEY.
Marriage. James Rosbrugh born. Ecclesiastical fidelity. Discouragements.   12

CHAPTER V.
TRANSITION TO ALLEN TOWNSHIP PENNSYLVANIA.
Letitia Rosbrugh born. Call to Allen Township. Negotiations for transfer to Allen Township Church. Allen Township Church transferred. Installation.   17

CONTENTS.

CHAPTER VI.
MINISTRY IN ALLEN TOWNSHIP PENNSYLVANIA.
Field of labor in Pennsylvania. Mirthfulness. Anecdotes.   21

CHAPTER VII.
INCENTIVES TO PATRIOTISM.
Patriotism. Synodical urging and admonition. Friends and neighbors enter army. Siege of Fort Washington. Washington's retreat. Excitement in Pennsylvania. Increased excitement. Heroic preparations. Families provided for. Schools and places of business closed. General Howe arrives at Princeton. Washington dictatorial. Washington's summons to Northampton.   25

CHAPTER VIII.
THE MARCH TO THE SEAT OF WAR.
Mr. Rosbrugh takes the decisive step. The patriotic sermon. Last will and testament. The military company formed. Arrival at Philadelphia and first letter to wife. Scarcity of salt. Commissioned chaplain. Colonel Siegfried commissioned.   38

CHAPTER IX.
ACTIVE MILITARY DUTIES AND DEATH.
Distribution of the American army. Preparing to capture Hessians. Washington's Crossing. March on Trenton. Battle of Trenton and capture of Hessians. General campaign. Plan of campaign. Favorable providence. The last letter. British move on Trenton. Battle of Assunpink. Circumstances leading to death. Mr. Rosbrugh killed. The burial. Ecclesiastical records of death.   46

CHAPTER X.
THE COMRADES AND BEREAVED FAMILY.
Preliminaries to the battle of Princeton. Americans arrive at Princeton. Battle of Princeton. Mr. Rosbrugh's company return home. Provision for soldiers' wives and children. Mrs. Rosbrugh's trials. Petitioning the Executive. Mrs. Rosbrugh granted redress. Orphans Court proceedings. Mrs. Rosbrugh's death and burial. Genealogical record of Rev. John Rosbrugh's descendants.   61

CHAPTER XI.
WILLIAM ROSBRUGH'S FAMILY.
Historical and genealogical record of the family, in the United States and Canada.   82

APPENDIX.
A. Thatcher family. B. "A relic of Northampton county." C. Robert Rosbrugh family.

MAP
To Illustrate Early History of
ROSBRUGHS in AMERICA.

JOHN ROSBRUGH,
CLERICAL MARTYR OF THE REVOLUTION.

CHAPTER I.
EARLY LIFE.

> The evil that men do, lives after them;
> But the good is oft interred with their bones.
> *Shakespeare.*

If illustrations were sought to prove that the reverse of this is true in many cases, perhaps no more suitable one could be found than may be drawn from the life and death of the one who is made the subject of this sketch, and whom we may appropriately designate CLERICAL MARTYR OF THE REVOLUTION. Amid all the light thrown upon his career socially, ecclesiastically and politically—by tradition and historical record—nothing but the good he did lived after him, whilst the evil was interred with his bones—so far as known no blot rests on his fair name.

Si:—"Dulce et decorum est pro patria mori."
If:—"It is sweet and glorious to die for one's country."

John Rosbrugh tasted of that sweetness, and had the patriot's glory. His unmarked grave deserves a tribute of respect from every true American who is in the enjoyment of the liberties which he died to secure. His name and record are worthy of a place, not only in the archives of written history, but in the thankful remembrance of every lover of human liberty, along with the other Revolutionary patriots who died that a nation might be born and live.

The records of many of his compatriots have long since been written, but these have been largely devoted to the perpetuation in memory of the courage and prowess through which these warriors were enabled to march to glory or death in the face of a foreign foe. This man's record is unique in that whilst he was a noncombatant, he met, we may perhaps truly say, the most cruel death of them all, in his efforts to subserve with them the great cause of American freedom.

We are then to trace the life and character of the man, not so much in the light of the soldier, as in the light of the patriotic and devoted citizen and minister of the gospel who shared the lot and died the death of the Revolutionary soldier. We are to make a record of the man's life and character as reflected by the motives which impelled, and the circumstances which surrounded him, in his career. It is to this task we now address ourself.

In order that his name may be correctly quoted and written by future generations, we first settle its orthography. This has been, in the minds of some, an unsettled question for nearly one hundred and twenty years. In the minutes of the Synod of New York and Philadelphia, between the years 1761 and 1777, it is spelled once "Roxburrow," once "Roxborough," and nineteen times "Rosborough." In the Reords of the College of New Jersey it is spelled "Rosbrough." Mr Headley in his papers on "The

Nativity. 3

Clergy of the Revolution," under date of August 12th, 1875, in the "*New York Observer*," wrote of him as "Rev. John Rossburgh." Rev. D. X. Junkin, D. D. in the same paper, under date of August 26th, attempting to correct Mr. Headley's orthography, spelled it "Roseborough." In Ellis's history of Northampton county we find it "Rosebury." We would state that there are still in existence letters written and signed by Mr. Rosbrugh, and his autograph may be seen also in the records of the Allen Township Presbyterian Church, of which he was the pastor at the time of his death. From these sources it is ascertained the correct spelling is "Rosbrugh." The name however, in latter years is by his descendants and other branches of the family, spelled "Rosebrugh," and so pronounced.

John Rosbrugh was not a native born American but belonged to that sturdy class known as the Scotch-Irish, who have furnished so large a proportion of the brains, backbone and muscle which have been indispensable in shaping and maintaining our nationality. He was of the number of those who, for conscience sake, left Scotland and went to the North of Ireland, and who have made that part of Erin's Isle present socially, religiously and politically so marked a contrast with its more southerly portion. He was born in the year 1714, shortly before the family left Scotland, or shortly after they arrived in the North of Ireland, the exact date of the migration not being now attainable. Of the family to which he belonged we have no definite information further than that he had an older brother, William. It seems that the same impulse which constrained the family to migrate from Scotland to the North of Ireland, impelled this William Rosbrugh, together with his brother John—though the latter was young in years—to take their departure for a land more inviting, beyond the sea, in America.

Just when they came to America is not now definitely known.

Collateral circumstances however, would point to the probable time at which they came. It was doubtless at the time those Scotch-Irish Settlements were formed in the Middle States, which figured so prominently in colonial history and the early history of our nation.

They settled in New Jersey, but in what particular part we are unable to decide. John's first marriage took place about the year 1733, when he was nineteen years of age. His wife's christian name was Sarah, but the surname has been lost. He has no descendants by this marriage, the wife dying at the birth of their first child, which also died at the same time.

For the next twenty-seven or twenty-eight years we have very little information with regard to the family. The elder brother William, died, leaving two sons, Robert and John. The latter, after his father's death, and until he was of age, made his home with his brother John, for whom he was called.

Abner A. Rosebrugh, M. D., of Toronto, Canada, is a descendant of William, the brother of the Subject of this sketch.

CHAPTER II.

PREPARATION FOR THE MINISTRY.

What private advantages Mr. Rosbrugh had for obtaining an education, is now unknown. He however pursued his studies in the College of New Jersey, at Princeton, graduating there, as the records show, in 1761 in the class with David Caldwell, Lawrence Van Derver, David Gillespie, Isaac Handy, Thomas Henderson, William Jauncy, Nathan Ker, John Lefferty, Thomas McCracken, David Rice, Samuel Sloan, Jacob Thompson and Jahleel Woodbridge.

What incentives constrained him to seek the christian ministry will now perhaps never be known, but that his attention was so directed the sequel shows. It seems also that he was not possessed of sufficient pecuniary means to obtain that thorough education which was required of those who would enter the sacred office in his day. But there was a beneficiary fund in connection with the College of New Jersey, and to this he turned for aid. The conditions upon which aid could be obtained from this fund settled the question as to the beneficiary's character and qualifications. On the afternoon of Oct. 3d, 1755, Gilbert Tennent and Samuel Davies presented the following report to the Synod of New York, convened in the city of Philadelphia.

"*To the Reverend Synod of New York,*

"The annual interest of the following donations was appropriated by the donors, for the education of such youth for the ministry of the gospel, in the College of New Jersey, as are unable to defray the expenses of their education, who appear, upon examination, to be of promising genius, Calvinistic principles, and in the judgement of charity, experimentally acquainted with a work of saving grace, and have a distinguished zeal for the glory of God, and salvation of men."

Following this was a list of thirty-four names, showing a subscription amounting to £357 4s 6d, the donors being residents of the mother country.

A Beneficiary.

This fund was placed in the hands of the officers of the College of New Jersey, at Princeton, and the Synod by committee, from year to year examined beneficiaries and disbursed the interest of the fund. From 1758, the year in which the Synods of New York and Philadelphia united, till 1765, no regular report was made to the united Synod of the disbursements of the interest of the fund. In this year however, the committee in charge of the same made a report covering the whole period. The record is as follows:

"The committee appointed to dispose of the money in the hands of the treasurer of New Jersey College, appropriated for the education of poor and pious youth, brought in a state of their accounts since the year 1758, which is as follows:

		£	s.	d.
1758, Nov. 23. Paid by the treasurer to Mr. William Tennent for the use of Mr. Leslie,	-	13	0	0
For Mr. Carmichael, - - -	-	14	15	1
1759, Nov. 23. To Mr. Carmichael, - - -	-	10	00	0
1760, June 11. To President Davies, for use of Mr. Blair,		20	00	0
1761. Aug. 3. To Mr. Rosborough, per order, -	-	30	00	0
1762, May 25. To do per order, -	-	14	00	0
1763, Aug. 26. To Mr. Robert Cooper, per order,	-	20	00	0
1764, July 5. To do per order,	-	13	00	0
" Nov. 13. To Samuel Leak, per order, -	-	40	00	0
		£174	15	1

Thus we see John Rosbrugh at Princeton College in 1761 and 1762—though well on in years—classed as a poor, pious, promising Calvinistic young man, giving evidence of a work of grace in the heart, and having a distinguished zeal for the glory of God and the salvation of men.

Licensure. 7

Having been received under the care of Presbytery, May 22d, 1762, as a candidate for the ministry, by Aug. 16th, 1763, he had so far progressed in his theological studies that the Presbytery of New Brunswick saw their way clear to license him to preach the gospel. This fact appears also in a subsequent record made with reference to it. On the forenoon of May 17th, 1764, there was inserted in the minutes of the Synod of New York and Philadelphia, convened at Elizabethtown, the following:

"The Presbytery of New Brunswick report that since our last, they have ordained to the work of the ministry, the Rev. Messrs. Amos Thompson, Jacob Kerr and Nathan Kerr; who being present took their seats in the Synod; and that they licensed Messrs. David Caldwell, Francis Pepper and John Roxburrow, to preach the gospel."

It is probable Mr. Rosbrugh further pursued his studies after his licensure, and at the same time exercised his gifts as a preacher. By December 1764, the Presbytery was so well satisfied with his qualifications that they proceeded to his ordination. A reference to the minutes will show that this took place Dec. 11th, 1764. It was reported to the Synod of New York and Philadelphia, convened in Philadelphia, on the afternoon of May 15th, 1765, as follows:

"The Presbytery of New Brunswick report that they have ordained Messrs. James Lion and John Roxborough to the work of the ministry, and that they have licensed Simon Williams."

The place at which Mr. Rosbrugh was ordained was the old

Greenwich Presbyterian church, now within the bounds of the Presbytery of Newton, in Warren county, New Jersey.

CHAPTER III.
FIELD OF LABOR IN NEW JERSEY.

In referring to the old Greenwich church, formerly known in the neighborhood as the Tennent or Brainerd church, we must not confound the building and locality with the present Greenwich Presbyterian church, though the latter has occupied its present site for more than a hundred years. The spot where Mr. Rosbrugh was ordained was a half or three-fourths of a mile to the south or southwest. Leaving Phillipsburg for New York by the Cen. R. R. of N. J. the traveler is brought by a journey of about five miles, to the Pohatcong creek. As he passes over the high embankment by which the cars are carried over the bed of the stream, if he will look to the south-east, his eye will rest upon the site of the original Greenwich church, which is but a few hundred yards distant. It stood upon what is known as the Reily farm, now owned by Hon. H. R. Kennedy. If the traveler will go upon the spot, he will behold a scene of marvelous beauty. To the south he will see the Musconetcong range of mountains, with the stream of the same name flowing at its base. To the south-west and west he will see a broken range of hills, stretching far away across the Delaware into Pennsylvania. To the north-west and north, across the Pohatcong creek, will be spread out the fertile valley of the Delaware, in Warren county New Jersey, and Northampton county Pennsylvania, the whole circumscribed by the Kittatinny or Blue-mountain range, twenty miles or more away. To the north-east and east will appear the valleys of the Pohatcong and Musconetcong creeks with the range of hills which separates them. Such was the scene that met the eye of John Rosbrugh in December 1764, when he repaired to the old Greenwich church to receive ordination to the christian ministry. Nothing remains of the log church in which he reverently knelt except the foundation stones, which have been built into a lime kiln, which may now be seen near by.

It is probable that at the time of his ordination, Mr. Rosbrugh entered upon regular pastoral labors in the congregations of Greenwich, Oxford and Mansfield Woodhouse. Although there had been more or less preaching at one or other of these points by various clergymen as missionaries or supplies by appointment of ecclesiastical courts, for perhaps twenty-five years previous, Mr. Rosbrugh seems to have been the first settled pastor—at least of the Presbyterian order—north of the Musconetcong mountains, in the bounds of what is now Warren county, New Jersey. These three points of his charge seem to have been the earliest localities in the region, from which the principles of the christian religion were disseminated. By following the early records from 1739 on, it will be found that preaching was supplied from time to time at Mr. Green's—then Green's Ridge—then Greenidge—then Greenage—and finally lower Greenwich, which meant the place where Mr. Rosbrugh was ordained.

Likewise contemporaneously, preaching was provided at "Mr. Barber's neighborhood, near Musconnekunk." "Mr. Barber's." was supplanted by the name "Mansfield Woodhouse," doubtless to correspond with the name of the township in which it was located, or to designate it as being at a particular woodhouse in Mansfield township. * This was some eleven or twelve miles above lower Greenwich, and like it, in the Musconetcong valley. The traveler taking the cars of the Delaware Lackawanna and Western Railroad, at Hampton Junction on the Central Railroad of New Jersey, and riding toward Washington, passes through the bounds of the old Mansfield Woodhouse congregation. As he leaves the station he will see in the valley below, surrounded by white tombstones, the present Musconetcong Valley Presbyterian church, which is one of the daughters of the original Mansfield Woodhouse church. As he sweeps around the point of the hill a half mile further on, he will see, across the valley, upon the hill side, two or three miles distant, the white tombstones in the graveyard where once stood the mother church. On arriving at Washington he will see as one of the most prominent buildings of the place, the present First Mansfield or Washington Presbyterian church, which is the other daughter. Repairing to the old graveyard just indicated, now lying a half mile south of him, he will see all that remains to call to remembrance the labors of the Revolutionary pastor there. No stone, we believe, now chronicles the burial of parishioner or friend during his ministry, but the western part of the burial ground is filled with nameless graves, by the side of some of which he doubtless stood and performed the last rites of christian burial for the departed. Standing here upon the side of the hill which separates the Musconetcong and Pohatcong valleys, a beautiful prospect is spread out before the eye. To the south and south-west, three or four miles away, is seen the irregular range of the Musconetcong mountain

---

* Two other petitions from the Towhships of Greenwich and *Mansfield-Woodhouse*, in the County of Sussex, both of the same purport as above; were also read, and ordered a second reading.—*Minutes Provincial Congress of New Jersey, Oct.* 12. 1775.

beyond the stream of the same name, whilst in the intermediate landscape are seen fertile fields, comfortable farm-houses and inviting groves.

Oxford, the other part of the charge, was near Belvidere, the county seat of Warren. In early days it was known as "Greenwich upon Delaware," "Upper Greenwich," "Axford's,"—which name may still be seen in the burying ground and heard in the community—and finally "Oxford." It is now known as the First Oxford Presbyterian church, Presbytery of Newton. Two miles from Belvidere, upon a little eminence, just where a small stream flows out from among the northern spurs of Scott's Mountain, we find the site of the original Oxford church. Standing at the modern church amid the graves of past generations, to the south-west, west and north, stretch out beautiful hills and vales in upper Northampton county, Pennsylvania, and Warren county, New Jersey. Following the range of the Kittatinny mountains as they are seen projected against the sky, the Delaware Water Gap soon comes prominently into view to the right, whilst the New Jersey foot-hills stretch away to the east in broken profusion. Little or nothing remains at the site of the church to call to remembrance the first pastor and the days of the Revolution. Thus we see Mr. Rosbrugh in 1764, practically in charge of all the interests of the Presbyterian church in that large and prosperous region now known as Warren county.

CHAPTER IV.

MINISTRY IN NEW JERSEY.

It was at Mansfield Woodhouse that Mr. Rosbrugh made his home. Whilst occupied with the regular duties of his charge, he was appointed from time to time to supply neighboring congregations. On April 16th, 1765, Presbytery appointed him to supply two Sabbaths between that date and the third Tuesday in October, at Upper and Lower Hardwick—now Yellow Frame and Hackettstown, respectively—in the Presbytery of Newton, Warren county, New Jersey. On May 29th of the same year, he was appointed to supply two Sabbaths at Deep Run, near Doylstown, Pennsylvania, twenty-five or thirty miles distant. On October 16th, 1765, he was again appointed to supply two Sabbath at Upper and Lower Hardwick—twenty to thirty miles distant. On April 16th, 1766, he was appointed to supply one Sabbath at Upper Hardwick and one at Bedminster—in Somerset county, twenty-five to thirty miles distant.

Having entered upon the full work of the ministry, he felt that he ought to take to himself again a wife. Belonging to the class known as the Scotch-Irish, it was most natural for him to seek a helpmeet from among those who were of similar origin. Some twenty miles away, in Allen township, in "Forks of Delaware," now Northampton county, Pennsylvania, had been for nearly forty years, a settlement of the Scotch-Irish. To the Irish, or Craig Settlement as it was called, therefore, he looked for a wife. It was not long till he had found and won the object of his desire. He became intimate with the family of James Ralston, an elder in the

Irish Settlement, or Allen Township Presbyterian church. The family was composed of the following members, we believe, viz: Samuel, John, Mary, Jane and Letitia. As living descendants of this family, among others, we might mention Rev. J. Grier Ralston, D. D., of Norristown and the Ralston families of the old Brandywine Manor Presbyterian congregation, Chester county, Penn'a. The wife of the venerable Rev. J. N. C. Grier, D. D., for forty years pastor at Brandywine Manor, was also a descendant. Mr. Rosbrugh married the daughter Jane of this family, and took her to their home in the bounds of the congregation at Mansfield Woodhouse. The time at which the marriage took place we have not been able to learn, but conjecture it was in the early part of 1766. He was absent from the meeting of Synod, which convened in New York, May 21st, of that year. We conjecture he silently rendered his excuse, whilst absent, in the words of Nehemiah (6:3) "I am doing a great work, so that I cannot come down."—I am getting married. In philadelphia, May 20th, 1767, he gave to Synod his reasons for the previous year's absence, and for aught we know, gave them as here indicated. On the 24th of April, 1767, there was born to him a son, whom he called James, doubtless for his wife's father, James Ralston. Between the time of his marriage and the birth of his son, we find him engaged in numerous labors beyond the bounds of his own charge. On October 21st, 1766, he was appointed to supply at Upper and Lower Hardwick the first Sabbath of December, 1766, and first Sabbath in January and February, 1767. April 21st 1767, he was appointed to supply two Sabbaths in May, at Lower Hardwick, fourth Sabbath in July at Upper Hardwick, and fourth Sabbath in September at Bedminster. These labors in May, outside of his own charge, together with the journey to and attendance upon the meeting of Synod in Philadelphia the same month, show the arduousness of the service he rendered.

We find Mr. Rosbrugh was a man careful to obey the behests

of the ecclesiastical courts which had jurisdiction over him. The Synod of New York and Philadelphia had taken steps to secure a fund for the propagation of the gospel among the poor. They had enjoined upon the members to make collections for the purpose. On the afternoon of May 22d, 1767—the Synod then being in session in Philadelphia—the members were called upon to render an account of their faithfulness in the matter. When the list had been completed, the following minute was made, viz:

"The Synod are obliged to declare that it is a matter of real grief to them to find that so many of their members have paid so little regard to the authority of Synod, enjoining a liberality for so pious and important a purpose."

Mr. Rosbrugh however, escaped this censure, for among the reports from the Presbyteries, the following came from the Presbytery of New Brunswick, to which he belonged, viz:

"Of New Brunswick Presbytery.

	£	s	d
Mr. Reed,	1	10	0
Mr. Hanna,	1	0	0
Mr. Kirkpatrick,	2	17	1
Mr. Rosborough,	1	0	0
	£6	7	1 Pro. cur."

Thus he appears as one of four, in his Presbytery, who were faithful under the injunction laid upon them.

On the 28th of May he obtained leave of absence for himself and elder, John Maxwell, from further attendance upon the sessions of the Synod at that meeting, and started upon his journey homeward. Having returned to his duties at home, he doubtless in connection therewith, performed the extra service in July and September, to which he had been appointed by Presbytery in the spring. We find that at the fall meeting of Presbytery, on October 20th, 1767, he was appointed to preach one Sabbath at Upper Hardwick and one at Smithfield—the latter being now within the bounds of Lehigh Presbytery, in Monroe county, Pennsylvania, beyond the Kittatinny range of mountains, twenty or thirty miles distant. We present these details of labor that an adequate idea may be formed of the arduous and patient services rendered by the subject of this sketch. Mansfield Woodhouse and Oxford were each ten or twelve miles from Greenwich, and five or six from each other. Remembering this, and also that in addition to the labor of serving these congregations under such circumstances, he traveled far and preached much in the regions beyond, we have some forecast of the indomitable courage, perseverance and devotion to duty which manifested itself in severer trials in after years. In all this work there was doubtless little encouragement, at least in a worldly point of view. The discouraging phase of his experience is reflected in a representation which he made of his charge to Presbytery on April 19th, 1768. The record is as follows:

"Mr. Rosborough represented to the Presbytery, that Mansfield Woodhouse, one branch of his present charge, through the removal of sundry of his members out of the congregation, and by other means were now become so few and weak as not to be able to contribute their quota towards his support, and that sundry of them had consented to his leaving them. And that seeing the other branches of his charge were not able to make up the deficiency of that now mentioned; and as his circumstances are straightened and necessitous, these things laid him under the disagreeable necessity of asking to be wholly dismissed from his present charge."

The consideration of this matter was laid over till the next day. It then came up and the following record was made with regard to it.

"Mr. Rosbrugh's request for a removal from his present charge, came under consideration, and the Presbytery after hearing and considering the reasons for said motion, do judge that the matter is not yet ripe for proceeding to his removal, as it does not appear to us that Mansfield Woodhouse, the branch of the congregation which it seems is most deficient in supporting Mr. Rosbrugh, have been formally notified of Mr. Rosbrugh's design at this time to sue for a dismission from them; neither is there any representative here to answer for them; neither is there any one here to represent Oxford congregation, which is another branch of his charge; and as the removal of a minister is a weighty matter, and not to be rashly done, we would proceed with all possible tenderness and caution in it. We therefore think proper to defer the matter till the fall Presbytery, and in the mean time order that Mr. Rosborough give due notice to the people of Mansfield Woodhouse that unless they discharge their arrears and pay their quota as usual, his labors shall be taken from them; and should they decline to bear their part as before, then Mr. Rosborough is to preach one half of his time till next Presbytery, at Greenwich, and a third part at Oxford, and the remainder at discretion."

Such was the status of his affairs in April, 1768. At the same meeting of Presbytery when the above action was taken, he was appointed to supply one Sabbath at Smithfield and one at Allentown, in the Irish Settlement, Northampton county, Pennsylvania, and preach as often as he could at Upper and Lower Hardwick, between that time and the spring meeting of Presbytery. At the fall meeting of Presbytery, October 18th, 1768, the report was brought in that Mansfield Woodhouse had failed to make up their quota of Mr. Rosbrugh's salary, and that he had accordingly preached one-half of his time at Greenwich, and one-third at Oxford. The Presbytery adjourned to meet at Oxford on the third Wednesday of

November to further consider the case. At this meeting it seems some arrangement was made and certain conditions specified upon which Mr. Rosbrugh was to remain in charge of Greenwich and Oxford. At the spring meeting of Presbytery however, April 18th, 1769, it was reported that Oxford and Greenwich had failed to comply with the conditions upon which he was to remain with them, and he was accordingly dismissed from all parts of his charge.

CHAPTER V.
TRANSITION TO ALLEN TOWNSHIP PENNSYLVANIA.

The foregoing circumstances would seem to indicate that the immediate future was dark and uninviting to the churchless pastor. But such was not the case. Within a week previous to the meeting of Presbytery at which he was released from his pastoral charge, his heart was cheered by the birth of a daughter. This happy event occurred April 12th. He called his daughter Letitia, doubtless after the mother's sister, Letitia Ralston. With the little boy James, two years old, and the babe, we may suppose he spent many happy hours. But another circumstance added much to the dispelling of any misgivings which he may have had for the future. At the same meeting of Presbytery when he was released from his pastoral charge, a call was presented to him to take charge of the Allen

Township Presbyterian Church, in connection with Greenwich. Thus he was to be provided with a home in the Irish Settlement, Northampton county, Pennsylvania, among the Scotch-Irish, the stock from which he himself had sprung, as well as his wife. He was now called to the congregation in which his father-in-law, James Ralston, was an elder, and his wife's family were members. This matter had been well forwarded before the meeting of Presbytery which convened to dissolve the pastoral relation at Oxford and Greenwich. March 29th, 1769, the Allen Township people asked permission of the First Philadelphia Presbytery—to which they belonged—to present a call to Mr. Rosbrugh of the New Brunswick Presbytery; showing that they had decided at that time, to call him. They were advised to secure, in connection with Mt. Bethel, as much of his time as they could. Mr. Rosbrugh had expressed his willingness to accept their call, as early as April 3d., and the following record was made in their church-book, viz.:

"The Rev. John Rosbrugh accepted the call to Allentown congregation, the 3d. day of April, 1769; that is to allow the congregation two-thirds of his time for * * * pounds per annum."

The contemplated arrangement then doubtless was to give to Greenwich one-third, and Allen Township two-thirds of the minister's time. With this arrangement in view, the matter was brought before the Presbytery of New Brunswick, where it was duly considered, April 18th, 1769, and it was decided to make such arrangement, provided the Allen Township Church was "regularly set off to the Presbytery of New Brunswick," it having been under the care of the Presbytery of Abington from 1751 to 1758, and from that time on, under the First, or old Presbytery of Philadelphia. In pursuance of the stipulation of the Presbytery of New Brunswick, the Allen Township people petitioned the Synod of New York and

Philadelphia, convened in Philadelphia, to set them off to New Brunswick Presbytery. The petition came up for consideration on the afternoon of May 23d., 1769, and the following action was taken, viz.:

"A petition from the congregation of Allentown, in the Forks of Delaware, to be taken from under the care of the First Presbytery of Philadelphia, and to be put under the care of the Presbytery of New Brunswick, was brought in and read. After the committee on behalf of the congregation and both Presbyteries concerned were heard, it appeared not expedient for the present to grant the prayer of the petition. But the Synod order the First Presbytery of Philadelphia to inquire more particularly into the state and connection of that congregation, and empower said Presbytery to set them off to the Presbytery of New Brunswick if it should appear expedient; or if it should appear more expedient to set off the congregation of Greenwich to the First Presbytery of Philadelphia, the Presbytery of New Brunswick are empowered to set them off."

Notwithstanding this delay, Mr. Rosbrugh doubtless devoted his time thereafter almost exclusively to Allen Township and Greenwich. This is confirmed by a record made October 19th, 1769, by the Presbytery of New Brunswick, which is as follows:

"That Mr. Rosbrugh be a constant supply to the people at Greenwich and Allentown, except 3d. Sabbath to Mt. Bethel, till our next."

At the spring meeting of his Presbytery, on April 17th, 1770, he was appointed to supply one Sabbath at Mt. Bethel, one at Oxford, one at Baskingridge, at Lower Hardwick one, and administer the Lord's Supper, in addition to his regular labors at Allentownship and Greenwich. In accordance with the action of the Synod in 1769, the matter of the transfer of the Allen Township Church to the Presbytery of New Brunswick, came up on the afternoon of May 21st, 1770, in the Synod of New York and Philadelphia, convened in New York, when the following action was taken:

"The First Presbytery of Philadelphia reported, that in compliance with an order of Synod last year, they had, in conjunction with the Presbytery of New Brunswick, inquired particularly into the state and connections of the congregation of Allentown, in the Forks of Delaware, and it is the unanimous opinion of both Presbyteries that it is at present most subservient to the interests of religion in those parts, for the Presbytery of New Brunswick to take under their care, not only the congregation of Allentown, but also the congregation of Mt. Bethel, both which are in the Forks of Delaware, and both which have been under the care of the First Philadelphia Presbytery. The Synod therefore order the Presbytery of New Brunswick to take both the said congregations under their care for the future."

The conditions upon which Mr. Rosbrugh was to be allowed to accept the call to Allen Township and Greenwich, were thus met. Notwithstanding this, he did not at that time express to Presbytery his acceptance of the call. This may have been owing to troubles which arose about this time in the Mt. Bethel church, which was doubtless to constitute a part of his charge. In October, 1771, he was appointed to supply this latter place on the fourth Sabbath of that month and administer the sacrament of the Lord's Supper, and preach three more Sabbaths at his discretion. At the spring meeting of Presbytery, April 15th, 1772, he expressed his acceptance of the call to the Allen Township church, but for some reason no preparations were then made for his installation. If we mistake not, Greenwich was not included in the call as accepted by

Mr. Rosbrugh in 1772. On October 13th, 1772, the Allen Township people renewed their request for his installation, which was "cheerfully complied with." It took place October 28th, 1772, at 12 o'clock. Rev. John Guild presided and preached the sermon. The other members of the committee of installation were Rev. John Hanna, Rev. Jacob Van Arsdalen and Rev. Samuel Kennedy.

CHAPTER VI.
MINISTRY IN ALLEN TOWNSHIP PENNSYLVANIA.

At what particular time Mr. Rosbrugh removed his family to the bounds of the Allen Township congregation in Pennsylvania, is now not known, but it was most likely shortly after the dissolution of the pastoral relation between himself and the churches to which he ministered in New Jersey. It is not probable that he remained long in the bounds of the Mansfield Woodhouse congregation after the unhappy state of affairs which we see existed there in the latter part of 1768. The most natural place to which we would expect him to remove as soon as he conveniently could, would be the Allen Township congregation, where his wife's people lived. There we may suppose he took up his abode therefore, in 1769 or 1770. After his removal there were born to him two daughters, one of whom he called Mary, doubtless after his wife's sister, Mary Ralston, who had died, a blooming girl of sixteen, November 20th, 1748, and whose body lies in the Allen Township burying-ground. The other he called Sarah, perhaps in memory of the deceased wife of his youth. Another son was born to him here also, whom he called John, doubtless after his wife's brother, John Ralston.

If the traveler will go to a little hamlet near Weaversville, in Northampton county, Pennsylvania, he will be surrounded by the scenery amid which Mr. Rosbrugh spent the closing years of his life. The purling brook still flows by. The old mill-site is still there. The rocky ascent of the highway up which he marched with his parishioners when starting to the seat of war, is still there. The old Allen Township stone church, erected in 1812 and '13,—now hidden by a wooden encasement—is there, within a hundred yards or so of the site of the building in which Mr. Rosbrugh preached. Just up the stream a few steps, is the old burying-ground where lie the remains of his wife, by the side of Barbara Hays, Mary Craig, Thomas Herron, Mary Ann Walker, Mary Lykens, Hugh Wilson, Mary Ralston,—his own mother-in-law—Jane Clendinen and Mary Hays, together with others whom he laid in the grave during his ministry there. Leaving the church and going eastward, the traveler finds himself upon the elevated highway along which Mr. Rosbrugh traveled week after week as he toiled in the work of the Master. Away to the south-east, south and south-west may be seen the Lehigh mountains, with the river of the same name flowing at their northern base. Here and there as the eye wanders over the landscape, may be seen ascending at Catasauqua, Allentown, Bethlehem and other places, the smoke of the iron furnaces of the Lehigh Valley. To the east and west stretch out the fertile and beautiful hills and vales of Northampton and Lehigh counties; whilst away to the north, against the sky, may be seen the symmetrical range of the Kittatinny or Blue mountains. Having gone a mile perhaps, a sharp descent in the road brings the traveler to Reuben Beavers. This was the home of Rev. John Rosbrugh in 1776, and the home of his sorrowing family after his death. Just below it was the old Ralston estate, and blockhouse or fort for the defence of the settlers prior to and during the French and Indian war. Such were the surroundings of Mr. Rosbrugh after he removed from New Jersey to Pennsylvania.

From his installation in 1772 onward for several years, he seems to have been quietly occupied with his ministerial labors. He attended the meeting of Synod in Philadelphia in May, 1774. He attended the meeting of his Presbytery at Bound Brook, April 23d, 1776, and was chosen Moderator. He also attended the meeting of Synod in Philadelphia in May of the same year. On October 9th, 1776, Presbytery appointed him to supply two Sabbaths at Mt. Bethel, and one at Greenwich. This however, was the last opportunity his Presbytery had of assigning him to duty.

Before proceeding however to the darkest and sadest part of his career, let us take a glimpse at the bright and cheerful characteristics of his nature. Mr. Rosbrugh was fond of mirthfulness, and was accustomed to entertain his friends with such anecdotes as the following:

At the first meeting of Synod in Philadelphia, two young clergymen attended on horseback from Virginia. On the way, arriving at a village, near night, they inquired for a Presbyterian, hoping to find lodging for the night. They were directed to the principal man of the place, the owner of a mill at which many were employed. He gladly received them—showed them great attention —had their horses taken care of and supper prepared for themselves. After a long evenings talk, instead of asking the young ministers to lead in devotions, he thought it would be a good thing to show them how well he could do it himself. His method was patriarchal. He first read a chapter in the Bible, which he explained to the family, then a version of the Psalms—lining it in singing—before prayer. This night the chapter in course was the fourth of Numbers, the fifth and sixth verses of which are as follows:

"And when the camp setteth forward, Aaron shall come and his sons, and they shall take down the covering vail, and cover the ark of testimony with it: and shall put thereon the covering of badger skins, and shall spread over it a cloth wholly blue, and shall put in the staves thereof."

"Badger skins" he read beggar skins. When he had finished reading, he turned to the family and said: There is nothing of particular importance in this chapter, it merely goes to show the blessedness of the gospel dispensation, for now each man can enjoy his religion under his own vine and fig tree, but then, just as soon as a man became too poor to pay his tithes, off went his skin to be used in covering the articles in the tabernacle.

Mr. Rosbrugh, in making his pastoral visits, once came to a widow living alone. He found her at her devotions and did not disturb her until she was through. She read the Scripture, then lined a Psalm as she sang it, before prayer. He asked her why she lined the Psalm, as there were none to hear her when she was alone. "Ah!" said she, "it is sa quiet I fain would 'dight my gab twice wi' it."

CHAPTER VII.
INCENTIVES TO PATRIOTISM.

These were Revolutionary times, and Mr. Rosbrugh was filled with the spirit of freedom. It was the heavy yoke, politically and religiously, which the Mother Country had imposed upon her people, that drove him and many of his class from the heather, hill and dale of Scotland, to their new homes in America. That the same yoke should be imposed upon them in their new home, seemed to him like the pursuit and oppression of the innocent and suffering by a natural enemy. Aside from this general incentive which fired his zeal, there were special reasons why he should be intensely interested in his country's welfare. The Synod of New York and Philadelphia, to which he belonged, at its meeting in New York on May 20th, 1775, had sent out by pastoral letter, burning words of christian advice and patriotism to all her ministers and congregations, in view of the disheartening aspect of political affairs. Beside urging recognition of God in all the trials of the hour, and to duly repent of transgressions; to respect their allegiance to the British crown so far as might be consistent with the securing of their just rights, politically and religiously; to abstain from lawlessness and excesses in social life, they said:

"Suffer us then to lay hold of your present temper of mind, and to exhort especially the young and vigorous, by assuring them that there is no soldier so undaunted as the pious man; no army so formidable as those who are superior to the fear of death. There is nothing more awful to think of, than that those whose trade is war, should be despisers of the name of the Lord of hosts, and that they should expose themselves to the imminent danger of being immediately sent from cursing and cruelty on earth, to the blaspheming rage and despairing horror of the infernal pit. Let therefore, every one, who from generosity of spirit, or benevolence of heart, offer himself as a champion in his country's cause, be persuaded to reverence the name, and walk in the fear of the Prince of the kings of the earth, and then he may, with the most unshaken firmness, expect the issue either in victory or death."

"Be careful to maintain the union which at present subsists through all the colonies. Nothing can be more manifest than that the success of every measure depends on its being inviolably preserved, and therefore, we hope that you will leave nothing undone which can promote that end. In particular, as the Continental Congress, now sitting at Philadelphia, consists of delegates chosen in the most free and unbiased manner, by the body of the people, let them not only be treated with respect, and encouraged in their difficult service, not only let your prayers be offered up to God for his direction in their proceedings, but adhere firmly to their resolutions, and let it be seen that they are able to bring out the whole strength of this vast country to carry them into effect."

Thus Mr. Rosbrugh would feel that he was under moral obligation, with all Presbyterians, to lend his aid to repel what seemed to him an unjust demand on the part of the Mother Country. These feelings which doubtless possessed his soul in 1775, were intensified when some from his own congregation and family connections entered actively into the task of repelling the enemy, both in the halls of legislation, and land and naval forces of the country. If we look into the old burying-ground in the **Irish Settlement**, Northampton county, Pennsylvania, we will **find this inscription**:

"Dr. Matthew McHenry died December thirteenth, seventeen hundred and eighty-three, in the fortieth year of his age."

If we look into the minutes of the Council of Safety of Pennsylvania, for April 13th, 1776, we there read:

"*Resolved,* That Doctor Matthew McHenry be, and he is hereby appointed Surgeon to the Provincial Ship Montgomery."

His father was Rev. Francis McHenry, and his mother Mary Wilson, daughter of Hugh Wilson, one of the oldest, most respected and influential citizens of the Irish Settlement. In the minutes of the same body, for September 24th, 1776, we read: "An order was drawn on Robert Trowers, in favor of Messrs Jacob Strowd, Neigal Gray, Abram Miller, Simon Dreisbach, John Ralston, Jacob Arndt and Peter Brinkhalter, members of Convention for Northampton county, 300℔ powder, and 600℔ lead for the use of said county." Thus we see Neigal Gray and John Ralston, who were members of Mr. Rosbrugh's congregation, and the latter his brother-in-law, actively engaged with the military affairs of the country. Further, with others, we find the following Irish Settlement names as connected with the Revolutionary service, viz.: Major George Nagle, Lieutenant Robert Gregg, Ensign William Craig, John Craig, John Boyd, Andrew Boyd, William Young, William Weals, Henry Epple, General Thomas Craig and Robert Brown, afterwards known as General Brown, and who was a Representative in Congress from Northampton county, Pennsylvania, for nearly twenty years after the Revolution. Captain Benjamin Wallace, who married Letitia Ralston, Mr. Rosbrugh's sister-in-law, also entered the conflict on the field of battle. John Ralston—brother-in-law also as we have seen—became a member of the Constitutional Convention which framed the first constitution of the Commonwealth of Pennsylvania, in 1776, by which the people were to have no longer a government of a Colonial character, but that of a free and sovereign State. He was a member of the Continental Congress and also, we believe, a member of the committee or convention which framed the Articles of Confederation. Thus Mr. Rosbrugh became more closely identified with the Revolutionary cause from considerations alike of an ecclesiastical, social and political character. As the conflict progressed, circumstances more and more conspired to arouse his patriotism. General Brown, and his brother-in-law Captain Wallace, with others, were sent to the front, and shared the the misfortunes of the war previous to the siege of Fort Washington. They were of the number of those put into that ill-fated stronghold by General Washington, with orders to defend it at all hazards—it was the forlorn hope. The enemy marshaled their forces and laid siege to the place. It was superiority of numbers and munitions of war, against courage and devotion to a just cause. On the 15th of November, 1776, Lord Howe, Commander-in-Chief of the British forces, made a demand for the surrender of the fort, under penalty of putting all to the sword if the demand was not acceded to. An attack commenced on the morning of November 16th, and continued till three o'clock, P. M., when a second summons was sent by Lord Howe for the surrender, the stipulations being that the garrison were to be held prisoners of war, giving up their arms, ammunition and stores, and that two field officers were to be sent to the British head-quarters as hostages. As further successful resistance was deemed hopeless, the troops surrendered, and Colonel Robert McGaw, of the Fifth Pennsylvania battalion—to which belonged the companies containing many of Mr. Rosbrugh's neighbors —and who was in command of Fort Washington, General Brown, (then First Lieutenant in Captain Rundio's company,) and Captain Wallace, with the others, fell into the hands of the enemy. The following was the form in which the summons and capitulation were made:

"The Commander-in-Chief demands an immediate and catagorical answer to his second summons of Fort Washington. The garrison must immediately surrender prisoners of war, and give up their arms, ammunition and stores of every kind, and send two Field-Officers to these quarters as hostages. In so doing, the General is pleased to allow the garrison to keep possesion of their baggage, and the officers to have their swords.

Agreed to:
    J. PATTERSON, Adjutant General.
    ROBERT McGAW, Colonel of the Fifth Pennsylvania Battal ion, Commanding at Fort Washington." *

The following is General Brown's parole, given in his captivity, a year later:

"We whose names are hereunder written, do pledge our faith and honor to General Clinton, that we will not depart from ye house we are placed in by the Commissary of Prisoners; nor go beyond the bounds prescribed by him; and further that we will not do or say anything contrary to the interests of his Majesty or his Government.
    ROBERT BROWN
On board of ye Ship Judith, December 10th, 1777." †

The effect of the disaster at Fort Washington upon the minds of Mr. Rosbrugh and his people may well be imagined. Now followed that hasty and disheartening retreat by the Continental army across New Jersey, with which the historian is familiar.

---
* Genealogies, Necrology and Reminiscences of the Irish Settlement, p. 258—By the Author of this Paper.
† Ibid p. 259.

No place of safety was found until they had crossed the Delaware and placed this turbid and ice-clogged barrier between themselves and the pursuing foe. With the fall of Fort Washington it was felt something must be done and done speedily to prevent the enemy from marching on and capturing Philadelphia, where the Continental Congress had been sitting. If we now transfer ourselves to the chamber in Philadelphia where the Council of Safety of Pennsylvania were wont to meet, and imbibe the political atmosphere which they breathed, we will be better fitted to appreciate the circumstances and feelings through which Mr. Rosbrugh was brought to his tragic end. The Flying Camp had been formed, equipped and forwarded during the summer of 1776. The Irish Settlement had furnished her quota therefor. The air was full of alarms from time to time. By November 7th, an express rider had been sent out "to Northampton and Bucks counties, to request the Commanding Officers of the militia to hold themselves in readiness to march to this city at an hour's warning." By November 11th, " In consequence of intelligence received that part of General How's army was making a move this way, the Council to get things in forwardness to make a defence, came to the following rsolutions, viz. : 1. That twelve expresses with horses be provided, to be in readiness to send. 2. That Col. Gurney and Mr. Kuhl be appointed to examine the state of military stores and arms in the State House and lock factory, and report to the board the state in which they shall find them. 3. That Col. S. Matlack be appointed to write a letter containing the intelligence received, to the Commanding Officers of the militia. 4. That Commodore Seymore, Col. Humpton, Capt. Blewer and Capt. Hazlewood, do review the whole naval armament and the artillery companies belonging to this State, to-morrow, and make report to this board, of the state in which they shall find them. 5. *Resolved*, That Col. Bayard be appointed to draw up a letter to Col. Kirkbridge, to view the fords of the river Delaware above the falls. 6. That Mr. Biddle be appointed to write to the Delaware State, and lower parts of New Jersey, and acquaint them with the intelligence received. 7. That Mr. C. S. Morris be appointed to write to Mr. Parr, Mr. Tilghman and Mr. Lukens, and order them to remove the public papers in their hands. 8. That Mr. Robert Irwine be sent for and directed to engage a number of wagons, in order to remove the military stores from this city to the country. 9. That Col. Mifflin be sent for and requested to assist in directing the mounting all the small guns that can be procured, on carriages, in and near the city, that are fit for that purpose. 10. Mr. Towers be directed to provide a larger quantity of musket cartridges than is now on hand, and employ as many people in making them as can be procured. 11. That the boom be fixed to the piers near Fort Island, without delay." November 13th finds the organized militia notified "to march to New Jersey." On the 14th "intelligence was received by express that several hundred transports had sailed from New York, and steered their course to the southward, and expected to be intended for this city; whereupon the Council wrote a circular letter to the Commanding Officers of the battalions of militia, earnestly requesting them to march their respective battalions to this city immediately." "The Board of war was requested to send for Captain Strohbogh and the company of artillery under his command, lately sent to Fort Montgomery, in New York Government." "*Resolved*, That Col. Bayard be requested to get ready immediately as many of his battalion as are necessary to guard the State prisioners to Lancaster and Reading. The Commodore was not to suffer any sea vessel to pass through the Chevaux-de-Frise. *Ordered* that Commodore Seymore do immediately station one of the armed boats belonging to this State, at or near Gloucester point, and exert their utmost vigilance in preventing all shallops from passing down the river." But matters became more critical. The last stronghold, Fort Washington, is taken, as we have seen, on the

16th of November. By the 18th, the Chester and Berks county militia are ordered to Philadelphia. The 20th finds the Bucks county militia also ordered to the city. The troops from Lancaster and York counties receive their marching orders by the 22d. Now the sphere of action widens. It is no longer the authorities of Pennsylvania alone who are moving for the defence of their soil, but the Continental Congress takes up the matter and cooperates with them. On November 23d, Congress takes action looking to the calling out of all the militia of the country in defence of the city where they had been sitting. Accordingly on the 25th of November we find renewed efforts on the part of the Council of Safety. They say "In consequence of a meeting with as many of the Field Officers of the battalions of the city of Philadelphia as could be convened, it was, upon consideration, agreed on to present a memorial to the General Assembly on the resolves of Congress with respect to calling out the militia, and on the present state of the military Association; and a committee of this board was ordered to prepare a draft of such memorial, to be delivered to the House tomorrow morning." The memorial was presented to the Assembly on the 26th, and the arrangement made seems to have been to bring pressure to bear upon the people's patriotism in the great peril of the moment, and thus obtain volunteers indiscriminately from the militia, for the reinforcement of the Continental Army. As an inducement to volunteer, one month's pay in advance was offered. We read November 27th, "Agreeable to the Resolution of Congress of 23d instant, respecting the calling out of part of the militia of this State, an order was sent down from Congress on Michael Hillegas, Esq'r., Treasurer to the Continent, dated the 25th inst., for thirty-five thousand dollars, for advancing a month's pay to each man who shall enroll himself to serve till the 10th March next, unless sooner discharged." To further urge and encourage the matter, the families of volunteers are provided for, as seen by the following action taken November 29th. "*Resolved*, That this Council will provide generously, and in the least exceptional manner they can devise, for the families of the Associators, who shall march into New Jersey to join General Washington, exclusive of their pay, out of such moneys as they have at their disposal, unless the House of Assembly shall, before that time, make the interposition of the board unnecessary." The following further action is taken November 30th. "*Resolved*, That money be sent immediately to the Colonels of the militia of Chester, Philadelphia, Bucks and Northampton counties, and city of Philadelphia, to supply the families of such Associators as go into actual service and may stand in need of the same; and that each battal'ion do choose two subalterns, substantial freeholders, who are to receive from the Colonels of their respective battalions the said money and distribute it amongst the said families, from time to time, according to their need, in the most discreet manner, for which money they are to account with this board." The same day "William Parr is directed to remove all the records and public papers in his possession to Lancaster immediately." " Capt. Newman is permitted to take one or two of the field pieces in the State House yard, and proceed with them and his men to the assistance of General Washington." On December 1st " Resolved, That Mr. William Richards and Mr. Matthew Clarkson be appointed to provide every necessary for accommodating the militia on their passage from here to Trenton; to have oars fixed to each shallop, and proportion the number of men each can carry." "Dispatched expresses to Chester, Philadelphia, Bucks and Northampton counties, to hasten the march of militia to reinforce General Washington in New Jersey." "*Resolved*, That Major Proctor do send fifty of his privates with proper officers, under the command of Captain Thomas Forrest, to General Washington without delay; that they are to take with them two brass field pieces belonging to this State, and Major Proctor is to lay before this board an estimate of stores, wagons and camp equipage necessary for that service, that they may be supplied without delay." December 2d., "*Resolved*, That it is the opinion of this board, that all the shops in this city be shut up; that the schools be broken up, and the inhabitants engaged solely in providing for the defence of this city at this time of extreme danger." December 3d. "*Ordered*, That the ferry-men of this city and Liberties, do immediately take over to Cooper's ferries all their boats, and the two large flat bottom boats belonging to this State, now at Kensington, under the care of Captain Benjamin Eyre, to transport the Maryland Flying Camp across the Delaware to this city. *Resolved*, That the members in General Assembly for the counties of Philadelphia, Chester, Bucks and Lancaster, be applied to immediately, to recommend proper persons in their respective counties to be employed by this board to hire all the wagons in their counties. *Resolved*, That this board will furnish any persons who may form themselves into a Troop of Horse, with a brace of pistols and broadsword; and it is recommended to the persons so forming a troop, immediately to choose their officers and prepare to march to join General Washington with all expedition in their power." December 4th. "*Resolved*, That Jacob Hinman and John Clew be permitted to continue at the old ferry, it being expected that troops from New Jersey will pass over to this city, and they may be wanted." The 5th finds expresses sent out " to call the militia, and hasten their march to join General Washington." The 7th brings heroic words of admonition. "*Whereas*, The safety and security of every state depends on the virtuous exertions of individuals in its defence, and as such exertions can never be more reasonable and necessary than when a people are wantonly invaded by a powerful army, for the avowed purpose of enslaving them, which is at present the unhappy situation of our neighboring states, and which may hourly be expected in this, therefore, *Resolved*, That no excuse ought to be admitted or deemed sufficient against marching of the militia at this time, except sickness, infirmity of body, age, religious scruples or an absolute order from authority of this State. *Resolved*, That it is the opinion of this board that every person who is so void of honor, virtue and love of his country, as to refuse his assistance at this time of imminent public danger, may justly be suspected of designs inimical to the freedom of America; and where such designs are very apparent from the conduct of particular persons, such persons ought to be confined during the absence of the militia, and the officers of this State to have particular regard to the above resolve and act accordingly, with vigor, prudence and discretion, reserving appeals to this Council, or a committee thereof, where the same is requested." In the Council, startling news is broken at 2 o'clock A. M., December 8th. "A letter was laid before the board from Col. Bayard to Mr. Andrew Hodge, dated at Trenton, 2 o'clock yesterday afternoon, informing that General Howe was advancing at the head of his army toward Head-quarters at Princetown; whereupon Commodore Seymore was sent for and directed to order all the armed boats to be dispatched to Trenton immediately to assist in removing the stores, and any other service they may be required." "Ordered that the several ferries over Schuylkill be put in a condition to give the utmost assistance to the citizens and others, who may have occasion to pass and repass in this time of danger." In the afternoon "Letters were dispatched to the Colonels or Commanding Officers of the several battalions of militia in this State, informing them of the movements of the enemy, and entreats them to march with their battalions to succor General Washington, and empowering them to impress wagons to assist the inhabitants of the country to remove their effects, if not to be had without." On the 9th "An order was drawn on Mr. Nesbit in favor of Philip Boehm, of Northampton county, for one thousand dollars, for the use of the militia of that county." It was also "*Resolved*, That our treasury and the books of that office be removed to Lancaster, and that a wagon be procured to-morrow morning early for that purpose." By December 10th, matters had reached such a crisis that General Washington took upon himself to order out the militia of Pennsylvania, without waiting for the sanction of the State authorities, and " The Council being informed by General Washington that he had given notice to the several Colonels of Bucks county militia without delay to march their men to Head-quarters, and as it appears to this board that the measures taken by the General are essentially necessary at this critical time, it is terefore—Resolved, That the Colonels or Commanding Officers of that county comply with the General's request without delay, any order of this board before, notwithstanding." The 11th brings the forcible impressing of citizens into the public service, for the defence of the city. "General Washington having applied to this board to give Major General Putnam all the assistance in our power toward throwing up works of defence for this city, which are absolutely necessary; and as many of its inhabitants have not taken up arms to defend it against the invasion with which it is now threatened, whose indispensable duty it is to contribute in some way to the common defence, therefore—*Resolved*, That all able-bodied men, inhabitants of this city and environs, do contribute their equal proportion of labor, either by themselves or their substitutes, towards raising the necessary works of defence, the persons so employed to have the same pay and rations as the militia in the field, and in case any person shall neglect or refuse to serve in his turn, the Commanding Officer, or such person as he shall appoint for that purpose, is hereby authorized to seize and make sale of the goods and chattels of the respective delinquents, to the amount of such sum as shall induce another person to perform the work in their stead; and it is recommended to the General to call forth the inhabitants to this service by regular rotation, in such manner as may most effectually promote the same." If the Colonels of militia, who had been ordered out, were not able to bring onto the field their whole commands, they were directed to forward as many men as they could, as is seen by action taken the 13th. "*Resolved*, That the officers of militia who can raise indiscriminately, out of any battalion or battalions, a number of men to join General Washington's army, are hereby fully authorized and empowered so to do; and it is recommended to all the said officers to use their best endeavors to forward this salutary business, agreeably to the Resolves of the Honorable House of Assembly of yesterday, for which purpose they shall be paid all reasonable expenses." On the 17th we find matters urged in Mr. Rosbrugh's county by the offer of advanced pay to those who would enlist to save the imperiled country. "An order was drawn on Mr. Nesbit in favor of David Dashler for 2000 dollars, to be paid to Peter Rhoads, Esq'r., of Northampton county, for the purpose of paying a month's wages advance to the militia of the said county." The same day it was—"Resolved, That it be recommended to General Washington to issue orders immediately for the militia of Bucks and Northampton counties forthwith to join his army, and to disarm every person who does not obey the summons, and to seize and treat as enemies all those who shall attempt to oppose the execution of this measure, and likewise every person in those counties who are known or suspected to be enemies to the United States." Accordingly General Washington sent from his Head-quarters in Bucks county, the following letter to Colonel John Siegfried of Allen township, where Mr. Rosbrugh and his congregation were located:

"Sir:

The Council of Safety of this State, by their resolves of the 17th inst., empowered me to call out the militia of Northampton county, to the assistance of the Continental army, that by our joint endeavors, we may put a stop to the progress of the enemy, who are making preparations to advance to Philadelphia as soon as they cross the Delaware, either by boats or on the ice. As I am unacquainted with the names of the Colonels of your militia, I have taken the liberty to enclose you six letters, in which you will please insert the names of the proper officers, and send them immediately to them by persons in whom you can confide for their delivery. If there are not as many Colonels as letters you may destroy the balance not wanted. I earnestly entreat those who are so far lost to a love of country as to refuse to lend a hand to its support at this time, they depend upon being treated as their baseness and want of public spirit will most justly deserve.

I Am, Sir, Your Most Obedient Servant:
GEORGE WASHINGTON."

CHAPTER VIII.

THE MARCH TO THE SEAT OF WAR.

The general excitement revealed by the foregoing records, in which Mr. Rosbrugh's community in common with others shared, together with the direct appeal which General Washington's letter made to the members of his congregation as residents of Allen township, where Colonel Siegfried lived, were enough to bring the patriotic pastor to definite action. He assembled his congregation and read to them the call for reinforcements. He reasoned with and urged them to action. Having ascended the pulpit in the old church he took for his text Judges 5 : 23, "Curse ye Meroz, saith the angel of the Lord; curse ye bitterly the inhabitants thereof; because they came not to the help of the Lord, to the help of the Lord against the mighty." Having finished the sermon he told the people he could die in the full faith of what he had preached, the next moment. He had intended to go with his people to the field of battle in his proper capacity of Chaplain, if they would consent to march to the country's rescue. After sermon the people expressed their willingness to go if he would be their commander. This was a position he had not thought of occupying, and in which he would be exposed to more danger than if acting as Chaplain. He desired therefore to consult his beloved wife before acceding to the people's desire. Thus the congregation separated for the day.

Let us now follow Mr. Rosbrugh to the home in the little hollow in Allen township. Let us look in upon the interesting family upon this cold December night. Here is the wife, with heart full doubtless, at thought of the trying circumstances by which they were surrounded. Her sister's husband was a prisoner of war, consigned to the tender mercies of the enemy. Some of her neighbors were sharing his hard fate. Her brother John was in Philadelphia devising means, with the other members of Congress, whereby their families might be protected from the cruelties of an invading foe. Here are the little children, James, Letitia, Mary, Sarah and John, the oldest only nine years of age, too young to appreciate the sad circumstances surrounding the parents. The father makes known to the mother the desire of the people that he should go to the field of battle as their commander. She knows that the position is attended with many dangers, and in view of the recent sad news, she knows not but that the husband might ere long be slain in battle or taken prisoner, as her brother-in-law had been, and what would then become of herself and these little ones. But the country called and none should refuse. The people desiring her husband to go with them—not as Chaplain but as commander—she said "Then go." The matter being now settled, let us look in upon the man of God as he puts his house in order as if foreseeing an early death. Let us follow his pen as he makes his last will and testament. Let us note his words of sorrow and manly devotion.

* " LAST WILL OF
   JOHN ROSBRUGH. }

In the name of God, Amen. December ye 18th, 1776—I, John Rosbrugh, of Allen township, Northampton county, and Province of Pennsylvania, being in perfect health, sound judgment and memory, through ye great and tender mercy of God, but calling to mind that my dissolution may be near at hand, and that it is appointed for all men once to die, therefore I constitute, ordain and appoint this to be my last will and testament, in ye form and manner following: In ye first place, having received many and singular blessings from Almighty God, in this the land of my pilgrimage, more especially a loving and faithful wife and five promising children, I do leave and bequeath them all to ye protection, mercy and grace of God, from whom I have received them, being encouraged thereto by God's gracious direction and faithful promise, Jer. 49:11 "Leave thy fatherless children, I will preserve them alive; and let thy widows trust in me." Secondly: I appoint my beloved wife and faithful companion, Mrs. Jean Rosbrugh, to be my lawful attorney to require, demand and sue for and by all lawful means and ways to recover all and singular, ye debts due to me either by bonds, bills, notes or book accounts or otherwise; and also I do will and

---

* Will Book No. 1, Northampton County Records, p. 149.

appoint my above attorney to pay all my just and lawful debts, to take receipts and give discharges as amply and fully as if I were personally present. And further I will and bequeath to my deceased brother's sons, Robert Rosbrugh and John Rosbrugh—to Robert ye sum of five pounds, and to John the sum of ten pounds, to be paid to them out of my estate, as soon as may be conveniently done after my decease. And as for the remainder of my estate, I will leave and bequeath to my beloved wife, Mrs. Jean Rosbrugh, and to my dear children; and it is my will that it remain undivided, to be used and improved for ye benefit of ye family, at ye discretion of my wife, until some material alteration may happen in ye family—that is to say, either her death, or if in process of time my widow should see fit to change her condition by a second marriage —then I appoint my executors to make a division, giving to her and to each of the children, such a part as they shall in justice and reason, judge proper, without any regard had to former customs or usages, but still regard is to be had to merit and circumstances of ye parties, and then I appoint ye executors to be the guardians for the children, but if she continue as my widow till ye children come of age, I desire that she, with the advice of ye executors, just give such a part to each of them as her circumstances will admit. And I ordain, constitute and appoint the Rev'd Mr. Alex'r Mitchell, my faithful and dear brother in ye gospel of Christ, and my faithful and dear brother in-law, Mr. John Ralston, to be whole and sole executors of this my last will and testament. In witness whereof I have hereunto set my hand and seal this 19th day of December, 1776.

JOHN ROSBRUGH. [Seal.]

Signed, sealed, pronounced and declared to be my last will and testament, in presence of us,

JOHN WALKER.
WILLIAM CARUTHERS."

The Military Company Formed.

The will written, we may suppose the father and mother retire for the night, but more to ponder than to sleep. The morning dawns and we see the father take his eldest boy, and with him ride over to the church, upon the faithful gray horse, which was to perform this accustomed service now for the last time. The people assembled at the church, but having been home with their families, and having more fully "counted the cost" of going to war, thus leaving their families in a manner unprotected, they hesitated to take the final step. The pastor having decided to accede to their request to take command of them if they would go, told all who felt it their duty not to enlist, to go home and take care of their own affairs and look also to the interests of those who went. At the same time he told all who felt as he did, that duty called to the country's rescue, to follow him. He now put a musket to his shoulder and marched out to the highway, and all fell into line and followed. The little boy James, rode the gray horse by his father's side till they passed over the brow of the hill, just east of their home, as we suppose. Then the father took him from the horse, kissed him and bade him go home to his mother, and be a good boy till he should return—he never saw his father's face again.

In this company, among the rest, were John, Robert, James and Francis Hays, sons of John Hays, who had immigrated to the Irish Settlement in Northampton county, from West-Donegal in Ireland, in 1732. The eldest son, John, had married Barbara King, daughter of James King of the Irish Settlement. John Ralston, member of Congress, also had married a daughter of Mr. King, named Christiana. Thus the two men were brothers-in-law to each other, whilst Mr. Rosbrugh was brother-in-law to Mr. Ralston.

The company doubtless marched eastward from the church, past Mr. Rosbrugh's home, till they came to the cross-roads at Jacksonville, in East-Allen township, where they turned southward toward Philadelphia. They doubtless crossed the Lehigh at or near

Bethlehem, and followed the old "Bethlehem road" to the city. Here they arrived probably on the 24th of December, 1776. The following from the minutes of the Council of Safety, December 26th, doubtless applied, at least in part, to them:

"Order drawn on G. Bickman to pay ten pounds seven shillings and sixpence, for victualing the first division of third battallion of Northampton county militia."

Thus in eight days from the time the Council of Safety issued their call for troops, Mr. Rosbrugh and his parishioners, as a military company, were upon the field ready for action. As Mr. Rosbrugh's brother-in-law, John Ralston, was in the city in connection with his duties as a member of the Continental Congress, with him the patriot pastor spent the night of the 24th of December. The next day, Christmas, he wrote the following letter to his wife:

* "My Dearest Companion:

I gladly embrace ye opportunity of telling you that I am still yours, and also in a tolerable state of health, thro' ye tender mercy of our dear Lord. The important crisis seems to draw near, which I trust may decide the query whether Americans shall be slaves or free men. May God grant ye latter, however dear it may cost. An engagement is expected in a few days. All our Company are in Philadelphia in health and in good spirits. They are under the command of General Putnam, and it is expected they will be ordered to ye Jerseys to-morrow or next day. I cannot write much at present, only that we have had some encouraging news from ye Jerseys, but whether true or false we cannot determine. My dearest creature, ye throne of Grace is free and open; I trust you have an interest there; it will be to your

---

* Genealogies, Necrology and Reminiscences of the Irish Settlement, by the Author of this Paper, p. 267.

interest and happiness to live near ye Throne; you will find ye way of duty ye only way of safety. Farewell for a while. Please to present my compliments to Stephen and Nancy † and to all ye children. Praying that God may pour out his blessing upon you all, this from your truly affectionate husband:

JNO. ROSBRUGH.

P. S. Last night I lodged with Jno. Ralston; he is well.

PHILADELPHIA, December 25th, 1776."

Whilst he periled his life for the common welfare, he was not unmindful of the particular needs of his own family and friends at home. This was manifested in the exertion he made to secure for them that prime necessity of life, salt, which it was difficult to obtain in those Revolutionary days, and of which there was a great scarcity. The great depot for this commodity was at Germantown. With regard to it we find such regulations as follows, viz.:

"*Resolved*, That the salt now in possession of the Council of Safety, be immediately sent to the Committees of the several counties in the following proportions, to wit: Philadelphia county, 80 bushels; Chester, 80; Bucks, 80; Lancaster, 100; York, 80; Cumberland, 80; Berks, 80; Northampton, 60; Bedford, 60; Northumberland, 60; Westmoreland, 60; more or less as the quantity in store may measure. * * * The Committees are to sell it to the people at the rate of 15s per bushel, and in no greater quantity than half a bushel to any one family. They are to make as equal distribution as they can, according to the necessities of the people, for which purpose they are to require a declaration of what quantity they are possessed of more than their just proportion of this necessary article, at a time of such very great scarcity of it." On the 23d of December it was "*Resolved*, That the salt to be sent to the

---

† Servants.

several counties of this State, be sold out to the militia only who go into actual service at this time, or to their families, in the manner directed in our resolve of the 23d inst., as sent to the Committees." In further carrying out of this design, on November 30th, it was " *Ordered*, That the proportion of salt belonging to this State for the county of Philadelphia, be immediately put into the hands of the Colonels or Commanding Officers of the battalions of militia of said county, to be sold out on the terms mentioned in our resolves of the 23d instant, to the militia who go into active service only." By the 9th of December it was " *Resolved*, That the regulations lately adopted by this Council concerning salt, be no longer continued, and that all persons shall be at liberty to import that article and sell it in such manner and such prices as they shall find voluntary purchasers." It seems that owing to the removal of the restrictions as to the price, or from some other cause, the commodity, by the 26th of December, was held by those who possessed it, at a price little short of extortion. On this day we are told Mr. Rosbrugh purchased a bushel of salt, for which he paid $60, [?] with a view of having it distributed among his congregation. He also possessed himself of a circular giving an account of atrocities perpetrated by British officers. On the evening of this day (December 26th,) he wrote to his wife with regard to the bushel of salt, and enclosed the circular relative to the atrocities of the British officers. In this letter he said also:

" I have received this afternoon a commission sent me by the Council of Safety, to act as Chaplain of Northampton county militia, and am now entered upon the duties of my office. Oh! that God would enable me to be faithful."

In the minutes of the Council of Safety, December 26th, 1776, the following record is found:

" Commission made out for Jno. Rosbrugh as Chaplain to 3d. battallion of Northampton militia.

Thus was he relieved of the command of the company which he mustered and led to the seat of war, and Captain John Hays assumed the responsibilities of this position. This turn of affairs is readily understood when we remember, as indicated above, that each of these men was brother-in-law to Mr. Ralston, member of Congress. Mr. Rosbrugh's duties were now those of Chaplain, not simply to the company which he raised, but to all those troops from Northampton county known as the Third Battalion of militia. On the same day that Mr. Rosbrugh received his commission as Chaplain, Colonel John Siegfried, to whom General Washington addressed his call for the Northampton county militia, was commissioned Lieutenant Colonel of the same battalion, the following being the record: "Commission filled for Jno. Sigfret, Lt. Col. 3d. Batt'n Northampton."

CHAPTER IX.

ACTIVE MILITARY DUTIES AND DEATH.

Whilst the foregoing circumstances were transpiring at Philadelphia, there were important operations going on at Trenton. The British were not slow to follow up the advantage they had gained by the fall of Fort Washington. The retreating Continental army had scarcely reached the Pennsylvania shore, when a column of the

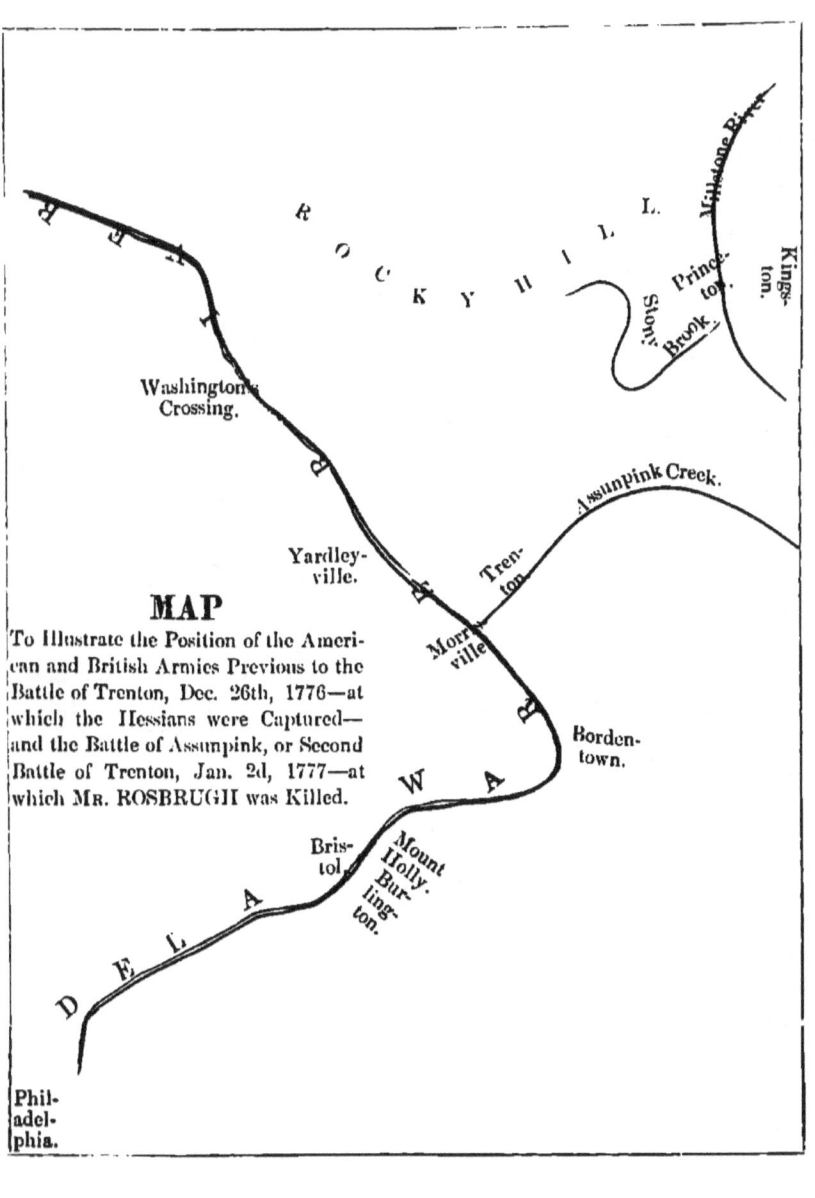

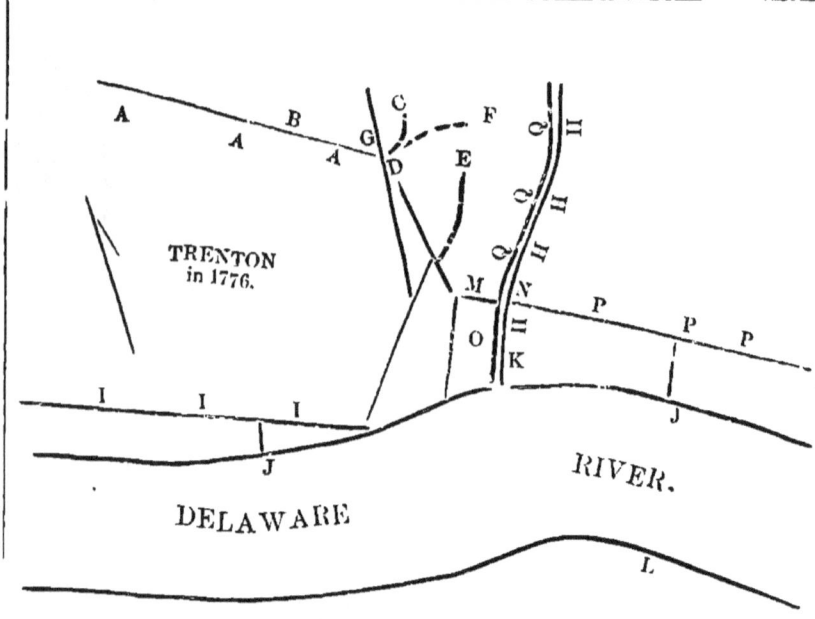

DIAGRAM. To illustrate the battle of Trenton, Dec. 26th, 1776—at which the Hessians were captured—and the battle of Assunpink, or second battle of Trenton, Jan. 2d, 1777—at which Mr. Rosbrugh was killed.

REFERENCES. A. Route of Washington and Pennington Road. B. Hessian outpost. C. Hand's rifle corps D. Captain Forrest's battery on King street. E. Point at which Hessians surrendered. F. Virginia troops. G. King street. H. American troops in battle of Assunpink. I. Water street—route of Gen. Sulivan. J. Ferry. K. Ford. L. Morrisville. M. Green street. N. Green street bridge. O. Spot where Mr. Rosbrugh was killed. P. Road to Bordentown. Q. Assunpink creek.

enemy occupied Trenton. The British army dared not attempt to cross the Delaware, filled as it was with floating ice, to pursue further their flying foe. They waited for the flood to subside and the waters to freeze, that they might thus have a natural bridge upon which to cross, crush their enemy, enter Philadelphia, and either capture or disperse the Continental Congress. This delay, to them, was dangerous, as the sequel shows. The army was conveniently distributed to await the opportunity for a forward movement. There were detachments at Burlington, Bordentown, Mount Holly and Black Horse, whilst divisions had been left at Princeton and New Brunswick. The special charge, however, of fifteen hundred Hessians and a company of British Light-horse, stationed at Trenton, was to watch the movements of the Continental army. Washington was eagerly awaiting reinforcements; but he divined that an opportunity would be afforded for striking an effective blow, upon the advent of the Christmas holidays. The Hessians were given to drinking and carousing at this time, and Washington felt that his opportunity was to fall upon them in the midst of their festivities and crush them when least prepared and least expecting it. The military forces by which this was to be accomplished, were variously distributed. The remnant of the Continental army was with General Washington, on December 25th, 1776, encamped near Taylorsville, on the west bank of the Delaware. The place was then known as McKonkey's ferry—or eight-mile-ferry—above Trenton. There were troops also, under General Dickinson, at Yardleyville, and some detachments encamped further up the river still. The Pennsylvania levies—the exertions for the forwarding of which we have already pointed out—were collected in two bodies at different points. One body was at Morrisville, directly opposite Trenton, under the command of General Ewing, or Irwine. The other was at Bristol, under command of General Cadwalader. General Washington's plan was for General Ewing to cross the river at or just below Trenton, whilst General Cadwalader was to cross still further down, on the night of the 25th of December, and thus cut off the Hessians from a retreat to the British troops stationed at Bordentown and Burlington below, whilst he would cross at McKonkey's ferry, eight miles above, and fall upon them from the north and east and cut off their retreat to the troops lying at Princeton and New Brunswick. Generals Ewing and Cadwalader however, failed in their part of the arrangement. On the morning of December 26th, General Cadwalader wrote from Bristol as follows:

* "Gentlemen:
There was a general attack to be made last night. The river was impassable here, and we made the attempt at Dunk's ferry, but found it impracticable to get over our cannon. We returned this morning to Bristol about four. I this moment have an account by Mr. McLane, (a man of veracity,) that he was at Trenton ferry this morning and heard a very heavy firing on the river and Pennytown roads, that lead to Trenton—the heavy firing lasted about one-fourth an hour and continued to moderate for about three-quarters. The Light-horse and Hessians were seen flying in great confusion towards Bordentown, but without cannon or wagons, so that the enemy must have lost the whole. A party of our men intercepted about a dozen Hessians in sight of our people on this side and brought them to the ferry and huzzaed. I have ordered the boats from Dunk's, and shall pass as soon as possible. We can muster here about 1800 men if the expedition last night in the storm does not thin our ranks. Has General Putnam crossed, and with what number? Pray, let me know, everything of this kind gives confidence to the troops. I have no doubt of the report, a heavy firing was heard at this place. An attempt was made to

---

* Pennsylvania Archives, p. 136.

pass at a little below Trenton ferry, but could not get over, that would have made the victory still more complete."

Later in the day he wrote:

"Gentlemen:

I wrote this morning to General Washington, directed to General Ewing at Trenton ferry, who informs me that he cannot yet ascertain the particulars of this morning's action. One wagon loaded with arms was brought down to the ferry (Hessian arms) and safely landed on this shore, and six Hessians. We have taken fourteen or sixteen pieces of cannon, a considerable of stores and clothing. The number of killed, wounded and prisoners is very considerable."

The same difficulty which General Cadwalader met, was experienced by General Ewing, as we see intimated in the above letter. Of this, General Washington also, said:

* "General Ewing was to have crossed before day, at Trenton ferry, and taken possesion of the bridge leading to the town; but the quantity of ice was so great, that though he did everything in his power to effect it, he could not cross."

These failures however, did not prevent General Washington from carrying out his part of the plan, and making the whole undertaking a success. † At McKonkey's ferry he had under his command on the evening of December 25th, twenty-four hundred brave and resolute men, and twenty pieces of artillery. As the shades of night closed in and shrouded their movements from view, these commenced to cross to the New Jersey side. If the traveler leaving Trenton by the Belvidere Delaware Railroad, will look out of the car window on the river side when the station "Washington's Crossing" is called, his eye will rest on the scene where this

---

* Historical Collections of the State of New Jersey, p. 293. † See ibid p. 296.

memorable event was enacted. Owing to the ice and other impediments it was near four o'clock in the morning, of the 26th, before all the men and artillery were safely landed. The men were, many of them, thinly clad and poorly shod, whilst snow and sleet were falling and the ground icy and rough. General Washington had been sitting upon a bee-hive silently awaiting the conclusion of the task of crossing the angry waters, but when it was accomplished, he gave words of encouragement and advice to his trusty followers, and took up his line of march for Trenton. Silence was enjoined upon all, lest they should be discovered by the enemy and their plan frustrated. Guides were sent ahead, in citizens dress, to obtain what information they could of the enemy's position. The troops marched in a body for about a mile from the river, when they arrived at the Bear Tavern; thence they marched down about three and one-half miles to the village of Birmingham. Here they halted and an examination was made of the condition of their firearms and ammunition. Alas! they found that the falling snow and sleet had wet their priming, and they were doomed, it seemed, to meet and fight the enemy at the point of the bayonet. At Birmingham the army was separated into two divisions, and it was decided to march the remaining four and one-half miles by different routes. One division, under the command of General Sullivan, took the river road. The other division under General Washington, accompanied by Generals Lord Sterling, Mercer and Stevens, took to the left and marched down the Scotch road until they struck the road from Pennington, about a mile from Trenton, and thence toward the town. So obedient had all been to the injunction of silence, that the enemy did not discover their approach until the guides came in contact with their out-posts in the edge of the town just at break of day. The challenge having been given and answered, and the discovery made that the Continental army was upon them, the sentries fired and retreated. The Americans now rushed forward and drove the out-guards into the town. Arriving at the head of King street, Captain Thomas Forrest planted a six-gun battery to sweep it. The enemy endeavored also to bring a battery to bear in the same street, seeing which, Captain William Washington, and Lieutenant James Monroe—afterwards President Monroe—rushed forward with the advance guard and captured the guns whilst the artillerists were in the act of firing. Part of the troops under General Washington marched down Queen street and bore off to the left, to cut off the retreat of the enemy in the direction of Princeton. The division under General Sullivan, which had marched by the river road, came in contact with the enemy in the south-western part of the town about the same time that General Washington fell upon them from the north. Both divisions of the army pressed the enemy, who gave no very serious resistance until they were driven through Second street, to a point near the First Presbyterian church. Here they attempted to make a stand, but it was of short duration. Finding themselves surrounded and overpowered, they surrendered. Colonel Rahl, their commander, was mortally wounded in the early part of the conflict, whilst endeavoring to rally his troops. He surrendered his sword to General Washington, after which he was taken to his Head-quarters, at the residence of Stacy Potts, on the west side of Warren, opposite Perry street, where he died. Owing to the failure of Generals Ewing and Cadwalader to cooperate with General Washington, the British Light-horse and some of the Hessians escaped, otherwise all the British forces in the place would have been captured. However, the result of the undertaking was a gratifying success, which greatly elated and encouraged the dispirited Continental army. General Washington immediately marched his prisoners up to McKonkey's ferry, where he took them across to the Pennsylvania side, and followed with his brave little army. Of the expedition he says in his report, dated Newtown, December 27th, 1776:

* "Finding from our disposition, that they were surrounded, and they must inevitably be cut to pieces if they made any further resistance, they agreed to lay down their arms. The number that submitted in this manner, was 23 officers, and 886 men. Col. Rohl, the commanding officer, and 7 others, were found wounded in the town. I do not know exactly how many they had killed; but I fancy, not above twenty or thirty, as they never made any regular stand. Our loss is trifling indeed, only two officers and one or two privates wounded."

Whilst this capture and landing of the Hessians upon the Pennsylvania shore, accompanied by the Continental army, was a success in one sense, it was doubtless in another sense, part of a failure to which Generals Cadwalader, Ewing and Putnam contributed by their inability to overcome the difficulties which confronted them, and which failure was afterwards retrieved only by the smilings of Providence. It was doubtless General Washington's design at this time no longer to remain on the defensive, but commence an offensive movement against the enemy. The capture of the Hessians, it would seem, was but the first stroke in the contemplated campaign. Of this design we have evidence in the communications above, from Mr. Rosbrugh and General Cadwalader. In Mr. Rosbrugh's first letter to his wife, written December 25th, it is said: "The important crisis seems to draw near, which I trust may decide the query whether Americans shall be slaves or free men. * * * An engagement is expected in a few days. All our company are in Philadelphia in good health and in good spirits. They are under the command of General Putnam, and it is expected they will be ordered to ye Jerseys to-morrow or next day." From this it will be seen that Mr. Rosbrugh and his company, with the others under General Putnam at Philadelphia, were virtually, if not actually, under

---

* Historical Collections of the State of New Jersey, p. 293.

marching orders on the 25th, and this could not have been with a view to assist in the capture of the Hessians, for this was to be attempted that very night. It could not mean otherwise therefore, than that they were to engage in a general campaign. The same thing is reflected by the words of General Cadwalader written at Bristol, the next morning, December 26th. He said "There was a general attack to be made last night. * * * I have ordered the boats from Dunk's and shall pass as soon as possible. * * * Has General Putnam crossed and with what number?" This implies that General Washington's crossing to Trenton was with the purpose of staying, as there would have been no object in the crossing of General Cadwalader after the battle, if all were to return to the Pennsylvania shore. His words also imply that General Putnam was to cooperate with him and Generals Washington and Ewing in a general movement. The plan of the campaign therefore seems to have been to concentrate a sufficient force at Trenton and below, to defeat or capture all the detachments of British troops at Trenton, Bordentown, Mount Holly and Burlington, and then mass against the heavier bodies at Princeton and New Brunswick. The capture of the Hessians was doubtless intended to be one of three or four simultaneous blows against the enemy on the night of December 25th. That against the Hessians at Trenton was successfully made, but owing to the inability of the other Generals to cross the river, General Washington made it single handed. If he had decided to remain at Trenton—send his prisoners and booty over the river— and await the crossing of Generals Cadwalader, Ewing and Putnam, the British forces at Princeton—nine miles distant—might have fallen upon him from the north, and those at Bordentown and below might have fallen upon him from the south, and crushed him before the reinforcements could have come to his relief. His discretion therefore, served him as the better part of valor, and he accordingly withdrew to McKonkey's ferry and recrossed the river.

The consternation that must have filled the British camp however, at the news of this bold and successful adventure on the part of the Continental army, can well be imagined. The next day, the 27th, that portion of the army lying at Princeton, pushed forward to Trenton and started in pursuit of General Washington. They followed up the Scotch road some distance and then crossed over to Birmingham. To their chagrin however, they soon learned that the Continental army had safely recrossed the Delaware with their prisoners and booty. Learning this, they returned to Princeton. But circumstances now conspired to bring on speedily a second conflict between the two armies. As Trenton was cleared of its British garrison, it would be a comparatively easy matter, under favorable circumstances, for the Americans to cross a sufficient force at that point to cut off and capture those troops which were stationed below at Bordentown, Mount Holly and Burlington, as was doubtless originally designed. This fact therefore would rouse the British officers to push forward from Princeton and New Brunswick all their forces as soon as possible to provide against further disaster and make amends as far as possible for the loss sustained at Trenton. Another circumstance transpired calculated to call forth all the energies of both British and Americans to accomplish the ends which they respectively had in view. When General Washington first crossed into Pennsylvania, early in December, he was careful to keep all boats and other means of crossing, out of the hands of the British. The enemy were deterred therefore from crossing by the openness of the weather and the tempestuousness of the river, added to the lack of means of transportation. This is clearly intimated by Washington's words in his letter to Colonel Siegfried of Allen township. But the storm of sleet and snow of the 26th, terminated in bitter cold. So cold did it become that before the captured Hessians and Continental troops could be crossed to the Pennsylvania side on that day, some of Washington's soldiers, it is said, were frozen to death. The river doubtless then became frozen over—for which the enemy had been waiting—and the natural bridge was thus formed for them to cross upon at any time or place and march upon Philadelphia. The same advantage was afforded for the Americans to cross their armies, which had been lying at Taylorsville, Morrisville and Bristol, and throw them between the detachments of the enemy at Bordentown, Mount Holly and Burlington, thus cutting them off from the main body at Princeton and New Brunswick. General Washington was not slow to make the most of this advantage. He proceeded to transfer the troops to the New Jersey side of the river, at Trenton. In doing this he would naturally hurry up all the troops in the vicinity, and it was doubtless on this account that Mr. Rosbrugh and his company, under command of Captain Hays, were sent in haste from Philadelphia up to Bristol. Accordingly we find him at Bristol ferry on December 27th. Here he wrote the following letter, doubtless on horseback, the brackets showing where the paper is gone. It is yellow and much broken.

* "[Friday] morning, 10 o'clock at Bristol Ferry, Decem[ber 27th, 1776.] I am still yours [but] I havn't a minute to tell yo[u that by God's grace our] company, are all well. We are going over to N[ew Jerse]y. You would think strange to see your Husband, an old man, riding with a French fusee slung at his back. This may be ye la[st letter] ye shall receive from your Husband. I have counted myself you[rs, and have been en]larged of our mutual love to God. As I am out of doors [I cannot at present] write more. I send my compliments to you, my dear, and children. Friends, pray for us.

    From your loving Husband,
          Jno. Rosbrugh."

---

* Genealogies, Necrology and Reminiscences of the Irish Settlement, by the Author of this Paper, p. 269.

This letter is addressed on the back: "To Mrs. Jean Rosbrugh, Delawr Forks." "The last letter." The words "The last letter," are no doubt in the handwriting of the bereaved wife. This is the last piece of writing known to have come from his pen. As we have already seen, the energies of the Americans were now directed to the concentration of their forces at Trenton. This doubtless went on with vigor between the return of the British to Princeton on the 27th, and the 2d. of January, 1777. By this time Mr. Rosbrugh, and the company he led out, with the others, had arrived at Trenton. Cornwallis, having hastened back from New York, whither he had gone to embark for England, supposing the contest in America was about ended, moved forward from Princeton and precipitated the battle of the Assunpink, or second battle of Trenton, which, to the British army, was one of the most bloody and disastrous of the many conflicts in which they engaged during the Revolutionary struggle. It was withal, one of the most important in its bearing upon the interests of American Independence, though it has ever been lightly passed over by the historian. Little do the many thousands of passengers, who travel over the Pennsylvania Railroad between New York and Philadelphia, think, as they halt at the Green street depot in Trenton, that they are upon the spot where was the thickest of the fight in the hotly contested battle of the Assunpink. Little do they think as they gaze upon the sluggish waters of the stream as they flow by that once they ran red with British blood. Yet such are the facts. This memorable conflict occurred on the 2d. of January, 1777. As might have been expected, the British at Princeton and New Brunswick were hurried forward with all speed, to retrieve as far as possible, the loss sustained in the capture of the Hessians on the 26th of December, by General Washington. Their exertions would be intensified by learning that the Continental army, largely reinforced, had crossed the Delaware and occupied Trenton. Having massed as heavy a column of

Battle of Assunpink.

troops as possible therefore, they pushed forward to Trenton, where they arrived on the afternoon of January 2d. General Washington, measuring the strength of the enemy, deemed it prudent to withdraw to the south side of the Assunpink, and take advantage of the stream and rising ground beyond, in receiving the onset of the foe. The withdrawal of the troops to this position we may well suppose was attended with some haste and confusion. The Americans had scarcely posted themselves ere the British, under Cornwallis, four or five thousand strong, came pressing forward to secure victory, before the sun should go down, by a contest which was intended by them to be short, sharp and decisive. Two points on the Assunpink were of strategical importance to them, and these they immediately attempted to secure. The one was the ford where Warren street now crosses, and the other was the bridge on Green street, near the Pennsylvania Railroad depot. * The enemy formed themselves into two columns, the one to force the ford at Warren street, and the other, the bridge on Green street. At the ford, it is said, they were repulsed with heavy loss, the stream being literally filled with their dead bodies. No better success attended their efforts on Green street. The Americans had planted as many cannon as could be brought into action, to sweep the bridge and street leading to it. Beside this the hill-side within gun-shot of the bridge was covered with infantry, to pour in leaden hail along with the cannon, in dealing out death to the enemy. The British came down Green street toward the bridge with the flower of their army in the van. When within about sixty yards of the coveted prize, they rushed to the charge with an exultant shout; but ere they gained the opposite bank of the stream, the American fire was so galling and destructive as to cause them to retreat in confusion. Now it came the turn of the Americans to send forth a shout of exultation, which

---

* See Historical Collections of the State of New Jersey, p. 301.

they did with a hearty good-will. Chagrined at the failure, and mortified by the exultations of their enemies, the British officers immediately reformed their ranks and rushed a second time to the charge. This time they were met by volleys of musketry and artillery redoubled in fury, and driven back again in disorder ere they had reached the middle of the bridge. Now another shout went up from the ranks of the Americans. Collecting their shattered ranks they again charged, but it was in vain. Their failure drew forth a final and long shout of triumph from the American army, and the battle of the Assunpink was over. Night now drew on and the two armies ceased their strife. Lighting their camp fires they awaited the fortunes of war upon the morrow. It was in the conflict of this evening that Mr. Rosbrugh lost his life. There have been various versions of the sad event. One is * "The heroic pastor was surprised in a farm-house near Pennington, by a straggling party of British troops, who finding he was a Presbyterian and a Whig, stabbed him mortally with their bayonets." Another is † "Having taken part in the capture of the Hessians [?] at Trenton, the first action in which they participated, the next morning Mr. Rosborough while in a farm-house near the village of Pennington, was surprised by a scouting party of British horse, and cruelly put to death." Tradition and history have handed down these with other statements in regard to it. The most trustworthy account however, is that which was given by Captain Hays, who buried the body, and which has been preserved in Mr. Rosbrugh's family. It was substantially as follows. We have seen that there was perhaps some confusion in the haste with which General Washington withdrew his army to the south side of the Assunpink, when Corn-

---

* Rev. D. X. Junkin, D. D., in address at 50th anniversary of the organization of the Presbytery of Newton, p. 29.

† Egle's History of Pennsylvania, p. 976.

wallis marched into the town. In the haste and confusion it seems he lingered behind the rest of his comrades. Seemingly not fully conscious of the dangers which surrounded him, he remained too long in the town ere he sought a place of greater safety with the army beyond the Assunpink. He came to a public house which stood upon the site now occupied by the Mechanics National Bank, corner of State and Warren street, in the city of Trenton. As night was drawing on, he tied his horse under a shed and entered the house to obtain some refreshments. Whilst at the table he was alarmed by hearing the cry "The Hessians are coming." Hastening out, he found that his horse had been stolen. Hurrying to make his escape by the bridge on Green street, he found, as we have pointed out, that cannon had been posted to sweep it and the guard was instructed to allow no one to pass; beside, those in charge of it were fast breaking it up. He turned his steps down the stream toward the ford where Warren street now crosses. On arriving there he found it impossible to make his escape. He then turned back into a grove of trees, where he was met by a small company of Hessians under the command of a British officer. Seeing that further attempt at escape was useless, he surrendered himself a prisoner of war. Having done so, he offered to his captors his gold watch and money if they would spare his life for his family's sake. Notwithstanding these were taken, they immediately prepared to put him to death. Seeing this, he knelt down at the foot of a tree and, it is said, prayed for his enemies. Now seventeen bayonet thrusts were made at his body, and one bayonet was left broken off in his quivering frame. Sabre slashes were made at his devoted head, three of which penetrated through the horsehair wig which he wore. So died the "CLERICAL MARTYR OF THE REVOLUTION," at the age of sixty-three, upon a spot now trodden by the busy multitude, and forgotten amid the hum and bustle of commercial life in the heart of Trenton. As the shades of that cold and dreary winter evening settled down upon the sad scene, his lifeless body became rigid in the icy embrace of death. The British officer at whose command he had been put to death, repaired to the house which Mr. Rosbrugh had so recently left, and there exhibited the dead Chaplain's watch, and boasted that he had killed a rebel parson. The woman of the house having known Mr. Rosbrugh, and recognizing the watch, said: "You have killed that good man, and what a wretched thing you have done for his helpless family this day." The enraged officer, threatening to kill her if she continued her reproaches, ran away as if afraid of pursuit.

It was not long until Captain Hays was apprised of the death of his pastor, upon which he hastily wrapped the body in a cloak and buried it where it lay, being under necessity to hurry forward with the rest of the troops in the night march which precipitated the battle of Princeton the next morning. Sometime afterward, Mr. Duffield, subsequently Dr. Duffield, pastor of the Old Pine-street Presbyterian church, Philadelphia, who was a brother Chaplain in the Continental army, took up the body and reburied it. The remarkable circumstance of fresh blood flowing from the body, is said to have attended the reinterment. There have been various traditions as to the place where the body rests. A common one is that it lies in the burying-ground at the Old First Presbyterian church in Trenton. Another is that the widow and her daughter went to the scene of his death to identify the body, and that the second burial took place at Father Cooly's grave-yard, a few miles from Trenton. This is highly improbable, as the oldest daughter was at this time less than eight years of age. Beside, the oldest son—then nearly ten years of age—in after years testified that he knew nothing of this journey on the part of his mother, or the burial at this place. Mr. Rosbrugh's descendants believe that the body was taken to Philadelphia, but where buried they have no means of ascertaining. The patriot pastor having been laid in his last resting-

wallis marched into the town. In the haste and confusion it seems, he lingered behind the rest of his comrades. Seemingly not fully conscious of the dangers which surrounded him, he remained too long in the town ere he sought a place of greater safety with the army beyond the Assunpink. He came to a public house which stood upon the site now occupied by the Mechanics National Bank, corner of State and Warren street, in the city of Trenton. As night was drawing on, he tied his horse under a shed and entered the house to obtain some refreshments. Whilst at the table he was alarmed by hearing the cry "The Hessians are coming." Hastening out, he found that his horse had been stolen. Hurrying to make his escape by the bridge on Green street, he found, as we have pointed out, that cannon had been posted to sweep it and the guard was instructed to allow no one to pass; beside, those in charge of it were fast breaking it up. He turned his steps down the stream toward the ford where Warren street now crosses. On arriving there he found it impossible to make his escape. He then turned back into a grove of trees, where he was met by a small company of Hessians under the command of a British officer. Seeing that further attempt at escape was useless, he surrendered himself a prisoner of war. Having done so, he offered to his captors his gold watch and money if they would spare his life for his family's sake. Notwithstanding these were taken, they immediately prepared to put him to death. Seeing this, he knelt down at the foot of a tree and, it is said, prayed for his enemies. Now seventeen bayonet thrusts were made at his body, and one bayonet was left broken off in his quivering frame. Sabre slashes were made at his devoted head, three of which penetrated through the horsehair wig which he wore. So died the "CLERICAL MARTYR OF THE REVOLUTION," at the age of sixty-three, upon a spot now trodden by the busy multitude, and forgotten amid the hum and bustle of commercial life, in the heart of Trenton. As the shades of that cold and dreary winter

evening settled down upon the sad scene, his lifeless body became
rigid in the icy embrace of death. The British officer at whose
command he had been put to death, repaired to the house which
Mr. Rosbrugh had so recently left, and there exhibited the dead
Chaplain's watch, and boasted that he had killed a rebel parson.
The woman of the house having known Mr. Rosbrugh, and recognizing the watch, said: "You have killed that good man, and what
a wretched thing you have done for his helpless family this day."
The enraged officer, threatening to kill her if she continued her reproaches, ran away as if afraid of pursuit.

It was not long until Captain Hays was apprised of the death
of his pastor, upon which he hastily wrapped the body in a cloak
and buried it where it lay, being under necessity to hurry forward
with the rest of the troops in the night march which precipitated
the battle of Princeton the next morning. Sometime afterward,
Mr. Duffield, subsequently Dr. Duffield, pastor of the Old Pine-street
Presbyterian church, Philadelphia, who was a brother Chaplain in
the Continental army, took up the body and reburied it. The remarkable circumstance of fresh blood flowing from the body, is said
to have attended the reinterment. There have been various traditions as to the place where the body rests. A common one is that
it lies in the burying-ground at the Old First Presbyterian church
in Trenton. Another is that the widow and her daughter went to
the scene of his death to identify the body, and that the second
burial took place at Father Cooly's grave-yard, a few miles from
Trenton. This is highly improbable, as the oldest daughter was
at this time less than eight years of age. Beside, the oldest son—
then nearly ten years of age—in after years testified that he knew
nothing of this journey on the part of his mother, or the burial at
this place. Mr. Rosbrugh's descendants believe that the body was
taken to Philadelphia, but where buried they have no means of ascertaining. The patriot pastor having been laid in his last resting-

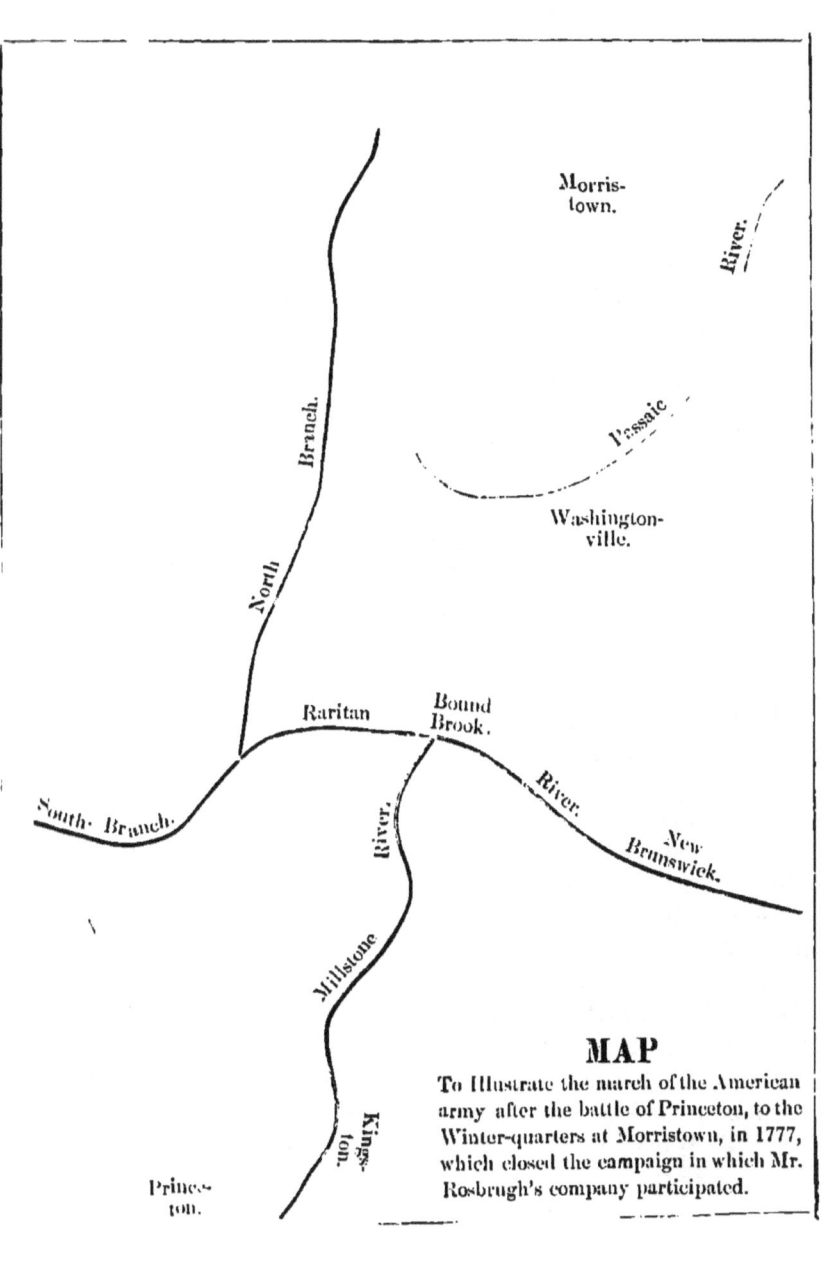

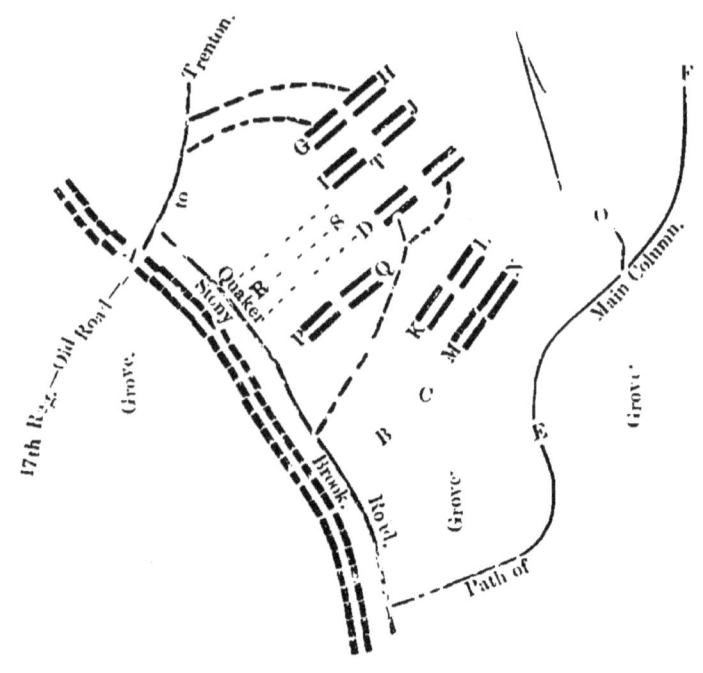

DIAGRAM. To illustrate the battle of Princeton, where Mr. Rosbrugh's company fought, January 3d, 1777. REFERENCES.
A. Bridge on old Trenton road, and Worth's mill, now owned by Mr. Joseph Brewer. B. Friend's Meeting-house. C. Thomas Clark's house, now the residence of Mr. Henry Hall, where Gen Mercer died. D. Where Gen. Mercer fell, mortally wounded. E. Head of column when first discovered by British. F. Head of column after Gen. Mercer's engagement. G—H. British 17th Regiment. I—J. Gen. Mercer's command commencing the action. K—L. British 17th Regiment formed to dislodge Cap. Moulder's battery. M—N. The Pennsylvania militia—doubtless including Mr. Rosbrugh's company—under Washington. O. Hitchcock's regiment. P—Q. Pursuit of Americans. R—S. Retreat of British. T. Where battle commenced, now the residence of Mr. Post.

place, on April 22d., 1777, the Presbytery of New Brunswick, to which he belonged, made the following record:

"Rev. Messrs. Tennent and Rosborough have deceased since our last Presbytery."

In like manner the Synod of New York and Philadelphia, of which he had been a member, convened in Philadelphia May 21st., placed on record the following:

* "New Brunswick Presbytery report, that the Rev. Mr. William Tennent departed this life March 8th., 1777; and that the Rev. Mr. John Rosborough was barbarously murdered by the enemy at Trenton on January second."

Thus his name disappears from the records of the church militant.

CHAPTER X.

THE COMRADES AND BEREAVED FAMILY.

Though Mr. Rosbrugh is laid in his narrow house, the tale has not all been told yet. Something remains to be said as to

---

† Records of the Presbyterian Church, p. 477.

the comrades and family whom he left behind. Doubtless Cornwallis, when he retired to rest on the evening of that ill-fated second of January, 1777, confidently expected the next morning to gain an easy victory over the insolent and derisive American army. But in this as in the attempt to force the passes of the Assunpink, he was doomed to disappointment. It was indeed a critical juncture in the affairs of the Continental army. The severely cold weather which had frozen the river subsequently to the 26th. of December, had now moderated. The ice was broken up, and in case of a defeat, there was no reasonable hope that the Americans could escape to their former place of safety on the Pennsylvania side. Furthermore the open weather had rendered the roads wellnigh impassable for artillery should a retreat be found necessary. But be the fate of the Continental army what it might, the city of Philadelphia was, at least for the time being, comparatively safe, as the swolen river would be as difficult for the British to cross now as the Americans. The bold plan therefore of Washington was to out-general his adversary. He conceived the idea of moving stealthily around to the rear of the enemy, and after defeating the detachment left by Cornwallis at Princeton, move on and capture the stores which had been accumulated at New Brunswick. As the strife ceased therefore on the banks of the Assunpink on the evening of January second, 1777, and the shades of night closed in upon the scene, a council of war was hastily held and this line of action adopted. Fences and other available material were freely used to make the campfires burn briskly, to lead the enemy to believe the Americans were quietly resting in their bivouac. Parties were set to work to dig intrenchments in the full hearing of the enemy's guards. Whilst this ruse was being kept up, when the proper hour came, and when the weather again turned suddenly cold, and the ground became sufficiently frozen to bear the artillery, the Americans silently folded their tents and stole away. A few were left to keep up the campfires among whom, it is said, were two or three of the Hays' from the company Mr. Rosbrugh led out. These were instructed to continue in this service till toward dawn of day and then retire. * Taking the route by Sandytown and over the Quaker bridge, by sunrise the next morning the army arrived at Stony Brook, a mile or two south of Princeton. The situation of the two armies was, at this juncture, anomalous. In the capture of the Hessians, when the British fancied Washington to be furthest away, whilst he was right upon them, contrariwise here, when they supposed the wily enemy was within their grasp upon the opposite bank of the Assunpink, he was far away, even at Princeton. On the morning of January 3d., 1777, at Trenton, the British commander opened his eyes to behold smouldering camp fires where had been the host which the night before dealt out death and defeat to his proud battalions. They were gone, but where! Not knowing what moment they might attack him from the most unexpected quarter, and with a mind full of amazement and bewilderment, a strange sound falls upon his ear. Can it be thunder from out a clear and crisp wintry sky? No, it is the voice of the enemy's artillery in his rear, and between him and his base of supplies. Cornwallis seeing that he had been out-generaled, faced about and rushed to the rescue at Princeton. Here the conflict grew fierce and bloody. The Americans having crossed Stony Brook, came to a grove of trees south of the old Quaker Meeting-house. Whilst the main body filed off to the right and directed their course toward Princeton, a detachment under General Mercer, composed of about 350 men, under the immediate command of Captains Stone, Fleming and Neal, marched to take possession of the bridge over Stony Brook on the old Trenton road. This was for the two-fold purpose of cutting off any who might attempt to escape to the main body under Cornwal-

---

* See Historical Collections of the State of New Jersey, p. 271.

lis at Trenton; and for the further purpose of protecting the rear of the American army against the pursuit of Cornwallis, which it was felt must take place within a few hours. Lieutenant Colonel Mawhood in bringing up the British reserves from New Brunswick, had quartered them in Princeton during the night of the 2d. of January. His command was composed of the 17th., 40th. and 55th. regiments, in connection with three troops of dragoons. On their march to join Cornwallis at Trenton, the 17th. regiment had crossed the bridge over Stony Brook on the old road to Trenton, before the near approach of the American army was discovered. Colonel Mawhood immediately turned back his command and as he recrossed the bridge, saw for the first time the detachment under General Mercer marching up the creek to secure possession of the bridge. The two detachments were only a few hundred yards apart at this juncture. Both now made a rush to obtain the advantage afforded by the high ground near by to the right. The Americans hurriedly advanced as far as what was then the house and orchard of William Clark, where they discovered the enemy coming up upon the opposite side of the rising ground. A worm fence was between the two lines, and to obtain possession of it both hastened forward. The Americans however, arrived first and delivered the opening fire of the contest. This was immediately returned by a volley and charge upon the part of the enemy, they being at the time only some forty or fifty yards distant. General Mercer's command, being armed only with rifles, were compelled to retire in disorder when but three or four volleys had been fired. General Washington hearing the firing, immediately led the Pennsylvania militia— among whom were doubtless the company led out by Mr. Rosbrugh —to the support of General Mercer. As the British 17th. regiment pursued the Americans under General Mercer, to the brow of the hill, they there for the first time came in sight of the whole American forces under General Washington. Somewhat daunted, they halted and hurried forward their artillery. General Washington had planted a battery, under the command of Captain Moulder, to deliver a raking fire against the enemy as they should advance. As they therefore pressed back the detachment under General Mercer, they were encouraged to attempt the capture of Captain Moulder's battery, but the galling fire which he kept up with grape-shot soon decided them to desist. This with the discovery that other regiments were leaving the main body and coming to the support of General Washington, caused them to flee precipitately across the fields up Stony Brook. The artillery which they had brought up was abandoned and fell into the hands of the Americans, but was of no particular benefit to them as they lacked horses to draw it off the field. The 17th regiment having been defeated and dispersed, it remained to engage the 40th and 55th. These made a stand in the hollow between the residence of the late Judge Field and the Theological Seminary. Overwhelmed here, they fell back and rallied at the college, many taking refuge within its walls. They soon found however that the day was lost. In this conflict the British lost over one hundred killed, and nearly three hundred taken prisoner. The Americans lost but slightly, perhaps not more than thirty killed and wounded; but among other valuble officers, the brave General Mercer fell, mortally wounded, in the early part of the engagement. General Washington having defeated all the troops that could render any successful resistance, detached a party to proceed to and break up the bridge over Stony Brook, on the the road to Trenton, so that Cornwallis would thereby be impeded in his pursuit. Scarcely had this party completed half their task, when the advance guard of the British appeared on the brow of the hill beyond, and opened fire upon them. They however bravely continued their work until the cannon balls began to fall thick and fast around them, and having rendered the bridge impassable, they retired. The artillery and baggage of the enemy were detained an hour or more here, whilst the other troops were ordered to dash through the stream—filled with ice though it was—and hurry on toward New Brunswick. Arriving at Princeton, they were brought to a sudden stand-still. General Washington had, among other things, captured a thirty-two pounder cannon, which he was unable to remove on account of its carriage being broken. When the Americans left, a few persons loaded this cannon, and when the British made their appearance, fired at them. They halted and deployed for battle, supposing that the Americans had resolved to make a stand in the town To their chagrin however, when they moved forward to take this artillery by storm, they found it deserted and no enemy in sight. By this ruse another hour was lost to the enemy. Meanwhile General Washington had hurried forward through Queenston to Kingston, on the Millstone river, three miles north of Princeton. Here a short halt was made and a hasty council of war was held, on horseback. The question was whether or not it was expedient, under the circumstances, to attempt to reach New Brunswick—some eleven or twelve miles distant—and capture the enemy's stores. The troops had fought in the battle of the Assunpink at Trenton, up to night-fall the evening previous; they had made the march from Trenton to Princeton during the night; they had been fighting and marching all the forenoon and had been deprived, to a large extent, of both breakfast and dinner; they knew that Cornwallis with his superior force must be near upon them in his pursuit from Trenton. If they attempted to reach New Brunswick in their tired and famished condition, they might be overtaken by the enemy and cut to pieces. Tempting therefore as the prize was, it was decided to file to the left at Kingston, toward Rocky Hill, and go down the valley of the Millstone, thus avoiding Cornwallis, who would be sure to push forward with all speed on the main road to New Brunswick. Thus closed up the scenes connected with the battle of Princeton, on January 3d, 1777. Scarcely had General Washington left Kingston when Cornwallis went by in hot haste toward his base of supplies, thus missing his wily enemy. As he passed over the hill beyond Kingston, owing to the rough and frozen condition of the roads, some of his baggage wagons gave out. These he left in charge of a few hundred men, and hurried on. During the night, some fifteen or twenty militia-men from the neighborhood, surprised the guards, captured the stores and took them to the American army.

From this time on, until the seventh of January — * by which time General Washington had arrived at Morristown—various were the trials and hardships of the Americans. The great object for which the Pennsylvania militia had been called out, was now accomplished. The enemy no longer threatened Philadelphia or any part of Pennsylvania's soil. He was in fact exerting himself to abandon even the soil of New Jersey. Under such circumstances, the company which Mr. Rosbrugh led out felt that their duty had been performed, and they accordingly left the army to return to their peaceful avocations at home, until the necessities of the country's cause should call them again to enter the ranks with their compatriots. They arrived in "Forks of Delaware" once more, on the 19th of January, 1777, passing through Bethlehem on that day.

But their return, whilst gladdening many hearts, brought bitterness and anguish to the bereaved wife of their patriotic pastor. His form was not seen among them, but cold and lifeless it lay in an unmarked grave by the waters of the Assunpink at Trenton.

Alas! bitter as this day's greetings were to her, it was but the beginning of sorrows. Mr. Rosbrugh's death was a sad calamity to his family. Although they were possessed of some means at the time of his entering the service of his country, before the Revolutionary struggle was concluded, they were reduced well-nigh to destitution through the loss of their natural protector and supporter,

---

* Pennsylvania Archives, p. 177.—General Putnam's letter.

and the financial distress which overtook the country as a concomitant of the struggle. They lost largely by the depreciation in value of the Continental currency, and alas! did not receive that sympathy and material aid which was due them from the officers of the law in charge of funds provided for those who became distressed because of the fortunes of the Revolutionary cause, until they were well-nigh driven to despair.

Although the authorities of Pennsylvania were busily engaged in the summer of 1776 in furnishing and forwarding their quota of the "Flying Camp," which was to check the progress of the enemy in their march to invade the Province, they were not unmindful of the necessities of the wives and children who were left behind by those who went to the country's rescue. With reference to the necessities of these we read in the minutes of the Council of Safety, July 15th, 1776, as follows:

"*Whereas* the Assembly of this Province did in a former session Resolve, That if any Associator, called into actual service, shall leave a family not of ability to maintain themselves in his absence, the overseers of the poor, with the concurrence of one Justice of the Peace of the city or county where such Associator did reside, shall immediately make provision by way of pension, for the maintenance of such family; and a true and proper account being kept thereof, shall be returned to the Assembly in order that the same may be made a Provincial expense, and paid accordingly. And as it is the opinion of this Committee that the funds of the said overseers will prove greatly insufficient whenever any considerable number of Associators shall be drawn into actual service, and that the administering to the wants of such families, by the hands of the overseer, will not be satisfactory to the Associators, or be likely to answer the good ends proposed, therefore

Resolved, That this Committee will, out of the funds of which they have the disposition, make such provision as shall be thought necessary to answer the said purpose, and that it be recommended to the Committee of Inspection and Observation of the city of Philadelphia, and the several counties in the Province to nominate and appoint a proper number of judicious persons residing in the said city and counties respectively, to distribute to such distressed families the allowance they shall judge reasonable. And that the said Committees be empowered to draw, as they shall see occasion, on this Board, for the necessary sums of money, to be by them lodged in the hands of the persons so nominated and appointed, to be applied as above directed, the said Committees to return accounts to this Board of the expenditure of the same."

The action thus taken under the auspices of the Provincial government, was accepted and ratified July 29th by the Council of Safety under the Commonwealth of Pennsylvania. The provision was carried into effect as may be learned by the subsequent acts of the Committee.

On March 20th, 1780, the Legislature followed up the commendable efforts of the previous four years in this direction, by passing an act for the relief of all such cases as were found to be worthy under the circumstances. This relief was to be afforded out of the funds accumulated from militia fines. Thus does it become manifest that those in authority honestly desired to alleviate the sorrows and necessities of those families who suffered from the loss of support consequent upon the service or death of husbands or fathers in the country's cause. Was not Mrs. Rosbrugh entitled to such consideration and relief? Had she not given up her husband to suffer one of the most cruel of deaths for the bleeding country? Was she not bereaved and needy, and were not her fatherless children destitute? Had not that Council of Safety, which provided for other's need, commissioned her husband to serve the common cause, and had he not fallen in the service to which he was assigned? Could she not then share in the common relief? Strange as it may seem, she was spurned and harassed almost to despair. She applied for relief under the act and received an order upon the proper authorities in the county of Northampton, for such aid as might be found necessary in the case, but was from time to time refused or put off with useless promises. When well-nigh discouraged, as a last resort, she sent the following petition to his Excellency John Dickinson, and the Executive Council of the state, under date of November 23d, 1784.

"To his EXCELLENCY JOHN DICKINSON, ESQUIRE; AND THE HONORABLE, THE EXECUTIVE COUNCIL OF THE COMMONWEALTH OF PENNSYLVANIA.

The Memorial of Jane, Widow of the Rev'd John Rosborough, late of Northampton county in said Commonwealth Most Respectfully Sheweth:

That your Memorialist's late Husband, the Rev'd John Rosborough, to encourage the militia of said county of Northampton to go out in the defence of their bleeding country, in the latter end of the year 1776, offered himself voluntarily to accompany them to Philadelphia, and there being solicited, duty and love of his country prevailed on him to accept a Chaplaincy in that arrangement of the American army composed of the militia of Pennsylvania; and a commission was accordingly made out, appointing him to that office. In his attendance on the duties of his office, he was inhumanly murdered by the enemy at Trenton, on Jan. 2d, 1777, and your humble memorialist left a wédow with five small children, in circumstances, tho' at that time somewhat good, yet now, by the inconstancy and fluctuating state of the late circulating currency, rendered very distressing.

A law being enacted by the Hon. Assembly of this state making provision for the families of those who fell in the defence of their country, your memorialist conceiving herself and children included in the salutary end and design of that act, did make application, but alas! she was frowned upon by the Prothonotary and denied relief. Your memorialist, after several fruitless attempts made, and as many repulses received, was advised to apply to your honorable Board as the dernier resort; unwilling to give trouble, yet impelled by necessity, she did, was graciously heard, and received a recommendation, signed by his Excellency the late President, read in Council, to those in office in said county, that upon her complying with the law in that case made and provided, she should be relieved. Full of hope, she returned, complied with said law, and made application again and again, like ye importunate widow, but met not with her success. Still turned off, with a promise of relief, yet never any received. To whom shall she complain of her wrongs? Or where shall your memorialist with her fatherless children look for redress of their grievances, but to your Excellency and Honors? Bear with her, necessity makes her clamorous; and the same makes her troublesome. She was made to hope that that law would yield her some relief. Your Excellency and Honors are the guardians of the law, and to you the oppressed and distressed flee for aid. If your memorialist is legally entitled to any benefit or advantage, to you she applies, that she may be directed, and orders given that she may obtain it. She submits her distressed case to your wisdoms, and entreats she may be heard, or conversed with on the disagreeable subject; and as in duty bound your humble memorialist shall pray always.

   (Signed,)
        JANE ROSBOROUGH.
 23d Nov., 1784."

This petition was duly considered and received the following indorsement, February 14th, 1785:

"See act of Assembly, pa. 365. Minutes of Assembly, 965."

"The case of Mrs. Roseborough and her family entitles them to such relief, agreeable to Act of 20th of March, 1780, as an Orphans Court of the proper county may think just and necessary, upon certificate from the overseers of the poor, of the necessity of granting them some support.

(Signed,)

JOHN DICKINSON.

Feb. 14th, 1785."

Having received Mr. Dickinson's indorsement, it came duly before the Executive Council, it seems, on the 27th of the next June, and was favorably passed upon, as the following indorsement shows:

"Read in Council June 27th, and an order drawn for £200 in her favor, p'ble out of militia fines. (See minutes.)"

From this source therefore, she received from time to time various sums, the amount of which, up to 1789, is shown by the following action of an Orphans Court, held that year:

"NORTHAMPTON COUNTY, L. S.

An Orphans Court held at Easton in and for the county of Northampton, the twenty-fifth day of September, in the year of our Lord, one thousand seven hundred and eighty-nine, before Peter Rhoads, Peter Kohler and Jacob Able, Esqrs, Justices &c.:

On the petition of Jean Rosbrugh of Allen township, setting forth that her late husband, the Reverend John Rosbrugh, having been killed by the British troops at Trenton whilst he was in the service of the United States as Chaplain to the third battalion of Northampton county militia; that the petition upon proof made thereof to the Orphans Court, obtained several orders for the relief of herself and family, as the widow and children of the said deceased; and by an order of the said court made on the seventeenth day of May, 1788, was to receive the full amount of the half pay of her husband from the time of his decease, deducting such sums as she had already received on that account; that the said account not being liquidated and the specified sum payable to her ascertained, she has not been able to avail herself of that order; praying that the court would please to settle and ascertain the amount payable to her, and grant an order for the same, and also to include in the said order the allowance to the present time.

At the same time the said petition presented the following certificate and account of the moneys by her received on orders made by this court, viz. :

We, * John Clyde and George Neihart, Overseers of the Poor of Allen township, Northampton county; and † James Clyde, William Moffet and Johannes Michael, Freeholders, inhabitants of the said township, do certify that Jean Rosbrugh, wife of the Reverend John Rosbrugh who was killed by the British troops at Trenton, is still a widow residing at the said township, with a family of five children, the eldest of whom is twenty-two, and the youngest thirteen, and that being deprived entirely of the support which they derived from the profession of Mr. Rosbrugh, and having suffered greatly by receiving part of his estate in depreciated money, and the widow advanced in years, we think it necessary that the relief intended by law for the families of militia officers, who were slain in the service of their country, should be extended to her.

Witness our hands this 19th day of June, 1789.

---

* The Author's great-grand-father, and after whom he was called.

† The Author's great-grand-uncle, and the father-in-law of the late Judge James Kennedy of Northampton county, Pennsylvania, who was the father of the late Dr. Clyde Kennedy, and brother of the late Judge Robert Kennedy of Stewartsville, Warren county, New Jersey.

JOHN CLYDE.   GEORGE NEIHART.   Overseers of the Poor.
JAMES CLYDE. WILL'M MOFFET.   JOHANNES MICHAEL."

"Account of moneys rec'd by Jean Rosbrugh, widow of the Reverend John Rosbrugh deceased, in virtue of orders drawn in her favor by the Orphans Court of Northampton county, viz.:

From Samuel Rea, Esq., Lieut, in Con'l money	£40 0 0
Rob't Levers, Esq., Lieut. and John Hays, Lieut.	15 0 0
David Rittenhouse, Esq., by order of Council at different times, paper money	300 0 0
	£355 0 0

September 22d, 1789.   JEAN ROSBRUGH."

"Whereupon the Court computing from the time the Rev'd John Rosbrugh was killed by the British troops, viz.: the beginning of January, 1777, to the 17th day of May, 1788, and calculated it to be 136½ months, and allowing the petitioner, Jean Rosbrugh, half pay of a Chaplain during that time—which is ten dollars per month—and will amount to   £511 17 06
Deducting thereout the above sum rec'd   355 00 00
                                                £156 17 06"

"Therefore the Court, upon consideration of all the circumstances, do decree and direct that an order be drawn on John Craig, Esquire, Lieutenant of this county, (this being considered as such) directing him to pay to Jean Rosbrugh, the widow of the Reverend John Rosbrugh deceased, out of the moneys appropriated by law for such uses, the sum of one hundred and fifty-six pounds seventeen shillings and sixpence, to be considered in full for the several allowances heretofore made her by this court, to the seventeenth day of May, 1788.   By the Court,

JOHN ARNDT, Clerk."

Such were some of the trials of Mrs. Rosbrugh consequent upon the death of her husband. She lived more than thirty-two years after his decease, dying March 27th, 1809. Upon her tombstone in the old Irish Settlement burying-ground, Allen township, Northampton county, Pennsylvania, may be seen the following inscription:

* "In memory of Jane Rosebrugh, who departed this life March twenty-seventh, eighteen hundred and nine, aged seventy years, relict of the Rev. John Rosebrugh, formerly pastor of this congregation, who fell a victim to British cruelty, at Trenton, January second, seventeen hundred and seventy seven."

"My flesh shall slumber in the ground
Till the last trumpet's joyful sound;
Then burst the chains with sweet surprise,
And in my Saviour's image rise."

Thus passed away the first generation, and it now behooves us to turn our attention to the descendants of Mr. Rosbrugh.

THE SECOND GENERATION.

Rev. John Rosbrugh's children were 1. James, 2. Letitia, 3. Mary, 4. Sarah, 5. John.

5. *John* was born, probably in the year †1776. He never married, and remained a resident of the Irish Settlement, Northampton county, Pennsylvania, at least down to the year ‡1810. The date of his death, it seems, is lost. Nothing definite either, appears to be

---

* Genealogies, Necrology and Reminiscences of the Irish Settlement, by the Author of this Paper, p. 201.

‡ Ibid, p. 276, Settlement Academy. See also History of the Allen Township Presbyterian Church, p. 183, by the Author of this Paper.

† See p. 73 of this Paper. He being the youngest child, we believe, is there certified to as being thirteen years old in 1789, which would put his birth in 1776.

Second Generation.

known as to the place of his burial, though tradition has it that he lies somewhere in Chester or Lancaster county, Pennsylvania.

4. * *Sarah* never married. She removed to Western New York, in the latter part of last, or early part of the present century, where she died at the age of seventy-six years. She is buried near Dansville, Livingston county, New York.

3. *Mary* married Robert Ralston, her cousin, who was the son of her mother's brother John, the member of the Continental Congress. They had an only child, a daughter, whom they called Christiana.

2. *Letitia*, born April 12th, 1769, † married Samuel Ralston, her cousin, son of her mother's brother Samuel. We believe they have no descendants. Her husband died January 11th, 1795, in the twenty-fourth year of his age. She never married a second time, but removed to Western New York, whither her brother, Judge James Rosbrugh had gone, in the latter part of last century. After living in widowhood about fifty years she died at the advanced age of nearly ninety, and was buried near Dansville, Livingston county, New York.

1. *James*, born April 24th, 1767, at Mansfield Woodhouse, now Washington, Warren county, New Jersey, is the only one of Rev. John Rosbrugh's children by whom the name in his branch of the family has been preserved. He remembered the scenes in Allen township connected with his father's raising the military company and their departure for the seat of war, and dictated these with other things, to one of his sons, before his death, by which means we have written testimony from him with regard to them.

When he had grown to manhood, ‡ he felt the need of a better

---
* Genealogies, Necrology and Reminiscences of the Irish Settlement, by the Author of this Paper, p. 128.
† Ibid p. 118.   ‡ Ibid, see p. 317 et al.

education than was afforded by "The Settlement," in which he lived, and began to look around for the means of obtaining the same. He could not leave his mother with his three sisters and a young brother to go to a distant school, consequently he must endeavor to establish a superior school in his own vicinity. It was necessary to raise money to build a house and hire a teacher. He went among his neighbors and friends and succeeded in getting the means for building a commodious stone structure, known to this day as "The Academy." If the traveler by the Lehigh and Lackawana Rail-road, going from Bethlehem to Bath, will look out of the car window to the east, when within about a mile of the latter place, he will see this building, which is still standing.

An accomplished teacher was employed and the project was a success, many receiving within its academic walls such advantages in learning as before could only be had by going away from home to a distant city. Many of its scholars were fitted for usefulness, some became distinguished—among others George Wolf, the celebrated Governor of Pennsylvania. When he went to old Mr. Wolf to get his subscription for the building and teacher, and to get him to promise to send George to school, he first met with a refusal. Mr. Wolf said George had already as good an education as he had, and he had done well enough. But, said young Rosbrugh, "dont you want to give George a chance to rise in the world? If he has an education he may become Governor of the State." Mr. Wolf laughed at the idea of his George being Governor, but he subscribed. George went to the school and became one of its best graduates. Having studied law, he became a member of the Legislature and subsequently Governor.

October 12th, 1792, James Rosbrugh married Margaret, daughter of Charles and Margaret McNair Wilson, of the Irish Settlement, Northampton county, Pennsylvania. Mrs. Margaret Wilson Rosbrugh was born May 15th, 1768, and died January 21st, 1857.

In the year 1795 the family removed to what was called the Genesee Country, in Western New York, arriving at what was afterwards their home—now Groveland, Livingston county—about the fourth of July.

Mr. Rosbrugh became naturally a leader among the people, acting as Justice of the Peace, and representing the great county of Ontario—which covered all the territory west of Cayuga bridge—in the State Legislature at Albany. During the war of 1812, he went home from Albany and raised a company among his neighbors as volunteers, was elected Captain and went with them to the frontier under proclamation of General Smith, who proposed an immediate invasion of Canada. Strange as it may seem, he here met, enlisted under the banner of the enemy, his cousin John Rosbrugh—William's son—who had visited him in his home in Western New York, twelve years before, as he journeyed with his family from New Jersey, to take up his abode in Canada.

He continued to perform his legislative duties at Albany, after the war closed, and was elected a member of the convention for the revision of the organic law of the state, in 1821. When Livingston county was formed out of Ontario, he represented it in the Legislature—was one of the county Judges, and also the first Surrogate—which latter office he held many years, and which terminated his public life.

He died November 18th, 1850, at his home in Western New York.

* THIRD GENERATION.

Aside from Judge James Rosbrugh's children, it seems that Rev. Mr. Rosbrugh had grand-children only through his daughter Mary, who married Robert Ralston. This daughter, as we have seen, had an only child, Christiana. She married Robert Neely, we

---

* With the third generation we adopt the modern spelling of the name, viz.: Rosebrugh.

believe. When she died, or where she was buried, we have not been able to learn.

The grand-children through Judge James Rosbrugh were as follows:

1. *Jane*, born November seventeenth, seventeen hundred and ninety-three, married William Leaming, May twenty-fifth, eighteen hundred and nineteen.

2. *John*, born October twenty-eighth, seventeen hundred and ninety-five, married Mary Gohene, September seventh, eighteen hundred and eighteen.

3. *Charles W.*, born May twenty-second, seventeen hundred and ninety-eight, married Maria Miles, June sixth, eighteen hundred and twenty-one.

4. *Hugh W.*, was born June fifteenth, eighteen hundred.

5. *James Ralston*, born July twenty-fourth, eighteen hundred and three, married Christiana Kelly, February sixteenth, eighteen hundred and thirty-one.

6. *Ezra*, born June tenth, eighteen hundred and seven, married Charlotte M. Bloss, February third, eighteen hundred and thirty-six.

7. *Margaretta*, born June twenty-fifth, eighteen hundred and nine, married Nathaniel A. Baldwin, May thirtieth, eighteen hundred and thirty.

FOURTH GENERATION.

The great-grand-children of Rev. John Rosbrugh, so far as we have been able to learn their names, are as follows:

THE NEELYS. If we have been correctly informed, the children of Robert and Christiana Ralston Neely were as follows:

1. *Washington*, of Findley, Hancock county, Ohio, who married Agnes Grier, daughter of Rev. J. N. C. Grier, D. D., of Brandy-

wine Manor, Chester county, Pennsylvania, and whose children are Oletha and Nathan Neander.

2. *John*, of Philadelphia, Pennsylvania, and

3. *Robert*, of Brandywine Manor, Chester county, Pennsylvania.

THE LEAMINGS. The children of William and Jane Rosebrugh Leaming were

1. *James R.*, born February twenty-fifth, eighteen hundred and twenty. He is Dr. Leaming of No. 160, West 23d. St., New York.

2. *Margaret*, born March twenty-third, eighteen hundred and twenty-two.

3. *Sarah*, born December first, eighteen hundred and twenty-four.

4. *Letitia Ralston*, born June twenty-third, eighteen hundred and twenty-seven.

5. *Thomas J.*, born May sixth, eighteen hundred and twenty-nine.

6. *Jane R.*, born March fourth, eighteen hundred and thirty-three.

THE BALDWINS. The children of Nathaniel A. and Margaret Rosebrugh Baldwin were

1. *Martha M.*, born March sixteenth, eighteen hundred thirty-one.

2. *Margaret R.*, born Aug. nineteenth, eighteen hundred thirty-five.

3. *Henry A.*, born Sep. thirtieth, eighteen hundred thirty-eight.

4. *Jane R.*, born Sep. thirtieth, eighteen hundred and forty.

THE ROSEBRUGHS. The family of John and Mary Gohene Rosebrugh, of Tecumseh, Lenawee county, Michigan, were as follows:

1. *Amanda*, born March sixth, eighteen hundred and nineteen.

2. *James*, born September sixth, eighteen hundred and twenty-one, resides at Amboy, Lee county, Illinois.

3. *Sarah*, born Feb. thirteenth, eighteen hundred and twenty-four.

4. *Anna M.*, born July thirteenth, eighteen hundred twenty-six.

5. *Chas., W.* born Aug. twelfth, eighteen hundred and thirty-one.

6. *Francis A.*, born May eighth, eighteen hundred and thirty-five.
7. *Margaret B.*, born May twentieth, eighteen hundred thirty-eight.
8. *Patience E.*, born Dec. fourteenth, eighteen hundred forty-two.

We believe one of the daughters of this family married P. C. Hosmer of Tecumseh, Michigan. Another married Clinton Blackmer of Cambridge, Lenawee county, Michigan. A third married A. D. Hosmer of Rochester, Olmstead county, Minnesota.

The family of Charles W. and Maria Miles Rosebrugh, of Freeport, Stephenson county, Illinois, were

1. *Henrietta*, born Sep. eighth, eighteen hundred and twenty-three.
2. *Caroline*, born Oct. twenty-eighth, eighteen hundred twenty-five.
3. *Letice R.*, born Aug. sixth, eighteen hundred twenty-seven.
4. *Ezra*, born May first, eighteen hundred and thirty-five.

The family of James R. and Christiana Kelly Rosebrugh, were

1. *Moses K.*, born March twenty-third, eighteen hundred and thirty-three. He studied law, married and settled in Ohio, where he died.
2. *Benjamin F.*, born February ninth, eighteen hundred and thirty-five.
3. *Daniel K.*, born January thirty-first, eighteen hundred forty.
4. *Christiana H.*, born September twelfth, eighteen hundred and forty-seven.

The family of Ezra and Charlotte M. Bloss Rosebrugh of Brighton, Monroe county, New York, were

1. *Amy Celestia*, born July fifteenth, eighteen hundred and thirty-seven, died May seventh, eighteen hundred and forty-one.
2. *Emma Jane*, born August tenth, eighteen hundred and forty-two, died August seventeenth, eighteen hundred and forty-two.
3. *Sarah Francis*, born August sixth, eighteen hundred and forty-

six, died July thirty-first, eighteen hundred and fifty-three.

Such are the links by which the present generation are bound to the Clerical Martyr of the Revolution, and the scenes connected with that dark page of American history.

CHAPTER XI.
WILLIAM ROSBRUGH'S FAMILY.

As intimated in Chapter first, the Rev. John Rosbrugh had an older brother, William, with whom he came to America. * Going back to the family history in the old country, we find that they left Scotland about the year 1720 and settled in the vicinity of Innis Killen, Ireland, where the parents died. In the family there were at least three children, viz.: William, John and Sarah. These immigrated to America about the year 1740. Of the sister's history we have not been able to learn anything. It seems they settled near what is now Dannville, Independence township, Warren county, New Jersey. The homestead is now, we believe, a part of, or adjoining the property owned by the Crane Iron Company, of Cat-

---

* Since the first chapter of this narrative was put in print, we have received through Abner M. Rosebrugh, M. D. of Toronto, Canada, a descendant of William Rosbrugh, and other sources, the more definite information given here. Note, that Dr. Rosebrugh's name is Abner M., as here given, and not Abner A. as given on page 4.

usauqua, Pennsylvania, and leased by Mr. William Vreeland of Danuville.

It was here doubtless, that Rev. John Rosbrugh spent his early life, and here that he married and buried his first wife. Here also his elder brother ended his days. The exact date of the death of William Rosbrugh, we have not been able to learn. It was however, sometime previous to 1776, a fact which is revealed by the provisions of Rev. John Rosbrugh's will with reference to his (William's) sons.

He married Jane Christie, who had a brother in Philadelphia engaged in mercantile pursuits. They both died a few years after their marriage, leaving three children, who were placed under the guardianship of their uncle, Rev. John Rosbrugh.

Those of the Rosbrugh connection who died whilst residing in New Jersey, were most likely buried in the old Moravian graveyard near Hope, in Warren county.

SECOND GENERATION.

The children of William Rosbrugh were Sarah, Robert, John. Of

1. *Sarah* there seems to be nothing now known. She probably died young and unmarried, an assumption which would seem to be substantiated by the fact that whilst the uncle, Rev. John Rosbrugh, their guardian, makes a bequest in his will to both Robert and John, no reference is made to their sister Sarah.

2. *Robert* married Isabella Carney or Karney.

3. *John* married Mary Carney, sister to Robert's wife.

When arriving at man's estate, the two brothers engaged in the milling business in what is now Hope township, Sussex, now Warren county, New Jersey. This property, we believe, is now known as Townsburry's mill, on the Pequest river, owned by Mr. John Green. They became possessed of considerable property, partly by inheritance but principally through their own industry.

Unlike their uncle, Rev. John Rosbrugh, they sympathized with the mother country in the Revolutionary struggle. At the commencement of the conflict, fearing the consequences of the course taken by the American people, and to protect themselves from the stringent measures adopted against such sympathizers—a few of which are hinted at in the foregoing pages—they sold all their property. The price was paid in Continental money which became well-nigh worthless at the close of the war.

Robert moved south, about the year 1783, and settled, it is supposed, in North Carolina. All trace of this branch of the family has been lost by those of the connection living in the north.

John's first wife, Mary Carney, died young, September sixth, seventeen hundred and eighty-six, leaving three children. He married, February fifth, seventeen hundred and eighty-nine, as his second wife, Susanna Thatcher, grand-daughter of Samuel or Elijah Thatcher, who is said to have been very wealthy, and who died in the city of Philadelphia.

Tradition has it that certain inducements were held out by the British authorities, for persons to remove from the United States to Canada, and that it was through this that John Rosbrugh removed his family thither, in 1800. On his way he visited for a few days with his cousin, Judge James Rosbrugh, at his home in Ontario, afterwards Livingston county, Western New York, who accompanied him one day on his journey, and endeavored to induce him to settle in Western New York. He was accompanied by the family of his first wife, together with the second wife's children, and they settled on a farm in the township of **West Flamboro**, two miles west of the town of Dundas, now the county of **Wentworth**, Province of Ontario.

In 1812 the two cousins met again, but then as soldiers, fighting under opposing banners.

*THIRD GENERATION.

The children of John Rosbrugh of the second generation, by his first wife, Mary Carney, were

1. *William*, born February fourth, seventeen hundred and eighty-one, and who settled in the township of South Dumfries, county of Brant, where many of his descendants now reside, their postoffice address being Branchton, Waterloo county, Canada.

2. *Sarah*, born June twenty-second, seventeen hundred and eighty-three, and who became Mrs. Griffin.

3. *Jane*, born January twenty-first, seventeen hundred and eighty-five, and who became Mrs. Turner. They settled near Erie, Pennsylvania, and were all believed to have perished by the burning of their dwelling.

The children of John Rosbrugh of the second generation, by his second wife, Susanna Thatcher, were

4. *Clorinda*, born April fourth, seventeen hundred and ninety-two, and who married Thomas Armstrong, who settled on a farm near St. George, county Brant, Canada West, now Province of Ontario.

5. *John Christie*, born September seventh, seventeen hundred and ninety-three.

6. *Thomas*, born October ninth, seventeen hundred and ninety-five, and who married Joanna S. Mulholland. They Settled on a farm upon which the present village of Branchton is situated, county of Waterloo.

7. *Robert*, born January fourteenth, seventeen hundred and ninety-seven, settled on a farm adjoining the town of Paris, Ontario, Canada, and died about five years since.

8. *Samuel*, born May fourth, seventeen hundred and ninety-eight.

9. *Abner*, born July thirty-first, eighteen hundred.

---
* With the third generation we adopt the modern spelling of the name, viz.: Rosebrugh.

10. *Mary*, born November thirteenth, eighteen hundred and two, and who became Mrs. Joseph Lyons.

11. *Susanna*, born May fifteenth, eighteen hundred and five, and who became Mrs. Hiram Hawkins. They settled in the town of Paris, Ontario, Canada.

FOURTH GENERATION.

The children of William Rosebrugh of the third generation, are William, John, and Enos, who reside at Branchton, Waterloo county; Hiram, Harrow, Essex county; Mary Ann, who became Mrs. Irving, Glenmorris, Brant county; Susan, who became Mrs. Dill, Drumbo, Oxford county; Sarah, who became Mrs. Pembleton, Oxford county; and Jane, who became Mrs. Inglis, London, Ontario, Canada.

The children of Mr. and Mrs. Sarah Rosebrugh Griffin of the third generation, are Mrs. William Buchanan, Branchton, Waterloo county, Canada. If others we have not learned their names.

The children of Thomas Armstrong and Clorinda Rosebrugh Armstrong are

1. *Thomas*, residing at Pontiac, Oakland county, Michigan.
2. *John*, residing at Goderich, Huron county, Ontario, Canada.
3. *Benjamin*, residing at St. George, Brant county, Canada.
4. *Samuel*, residing at Middleville, Michigan.

The children of Thomas and Joanna S. Mulholland Rosebrugh of the third generation are

1. *William*, residing at Rosebrugh's Mills, near Fayetteville, North Carolina.
2. *John W.*, M. D., Hamilton, Ontario, Canada.
3. *Abner M.*, M. D., oculist and aurist, Toronto, Ontario, Canada.
4. *Eliza*, who became Mrs. Knox, residing at Oakland, California.

5. *Eunice*, who became Mrs. Sylvester Smith, and who resides at Austin, Mower county, Minnesota.

6. *Mary*, who became Mrs. M. C. Moe, residing at Rochester, Olmstead county, Minnesota.

7. *Annie*, who became Mrs. C. C. Wilson, and who resides also at Rochester, Olmstead county, Minnesota.

8. *Susanna*, residing at Fayetteville, North Carolina.

The children of Robert Rosebrugh of the third generation were 1. *Hiram*, residing at Selton, and 2. *William*, residing at Bothwell, Kent county; 3. *Mrs. Hill*, Paris; 4. *Mrs. Collins*, Wyoming, Ontario, Canada; 5. *Mrs. McKay* and 6. *Mrs. Lorilla*, Chicago, Illinois.

The children of Samuel of the third generation are 1. *George*, and 2. *Rachel*, Drumbo; 3. *Mrs. Quackenbush*, Dundas; 4. *Emerson* and 5. *Daniel*, Harwick; and 6. *Mrs. Susanna Thatcher*, Chatham, Canada.

The children of Abner of the third generation, are 1. *Frank*, at Detroit, Michigan, and 2. *Melvin M.*, at Toronto, Canada.

The children of Joseph and Mary Rosebrugh Lyons of the third generation, are 1. *Sarah*, who became Mrs. Jarvis Bronte; 2. *James*, Ayr, Waterloo county; 3. *Susan*, who became Mrs. Henry Englehart, Burlington, all in Canada; 4. *John* and 5. *Ellen*, who became the wife of Hector Holmes, Owatona, Minnesota; 6. *Jane*, 7. *Harker* and 8. *Elsie Ann*, who became the wife of Daniel Vaughan, all of Lansing, Minnesota.

The children of Hiram and Susanna Rosebrugh Hawkins of the third generation, are 1. *Hiram*, at Bradford, Pennsylvania, and 2. *Joseph L.*, residing at Ottawa, Franklin county, Kansas.

3. *Mrs. Wm. Fonger*. and 4. *Mrs. W. H. Howard*, of Burford, Ontario, Canada. 5. *Mrs. W. H. Robinson*, residing at Suisan City, California. 6. *Mrs. Edson Marlatt*, residing at Paris, Canada.

FIFTH GENERATION.

The children of Thomas Armstrong of the fourth generation, are
1. *Alfred*, 2. *Charles*, 3. *Eunice*, who became Mrs. Collingwood, residing at Pontiac, Oakland county, Michigan. 4. *Clorinda*, who became Mrs. R. Furniss, of Clifton, Niagara Falls.

The children of John Armstrong of the fourth generation, reside at Goderich, Huron county, Ontario, Canada.

The children of Benjamin Armstrong of the fourth generation, reside at, St. George, Brant county, Canada.

The surviving children of Mr. and Mrs. Eliza Rosebrugh Knox of the fourth generation, are

1. *George W.*, who is a barrister, residing at Dixon, Solano county, California.

Thomas R., who is an official reporter, residing at No. 1416, Castro St., Oakland, California.

The children of Mrs. Jarvis Bronte of the fourth generation, are James, Milton, Halton county; Charles, Watertown; William, Burlington; Mrs. M. Richardson, Hamilton; Mrs. Amos Cassidy, Hagarsville, and Mrs. Samuel Magill, Nelson, all in the vicinity of Hamilton, Canada.

The only child of *Mrs. Sylvester Smith* is Fay Smith, banker, Austin, Minnesota.

APPENDIX.

A

THE THATCHERS.

As we have seen, page 84, William Rosbrugh's son John, married, Feb. 5th, 1789, as his second wife, Susanna Thatcher, grand-daughter of Samuel or Elijah Thatcher.

The old Thatcher homestead was in the Pohatcong valley, Warren county, N. J., eight or nine miles from Easton, Pa. It lay at the northern base of the range of hills which lie between the Pohatcong and Musconetcong creeks. Standing at the ancient residence and looking to the north, the eye falls upon a beautiful landscape, filled with fertile fields and inviting homes. In the midst of the valley is seen the Morris and Essex division of the Delaware, Lackawana and Western Railroad; at the further side, against the hills, is seen the Morris Canal; to the left lies Newvillage, whilst in front and near at hand is Broadway; then stretching far to the east and west is seen the enchanting valley of the Pohatcong.

The Thatcher family in early days were ardent adherents of the Methodist church. The old homestead was long famous as a place for holding camp-meetings. A stone church was built, which is now dismanteled and fast crumbling into ruins. It stands in a cultivated field, a hundred yards or so from the public road. Near by is the old Thatcher burying-ground, protected by a substantial stone wall, erected by the present generation who have descended from those whose bones rest there. Here doubtless are buried the first of the family who came to the region, but no inscription remains to designate their resting place. Of the family we have gathered the following items of information.

It seems the original Elijah or Samuel Thatcher had at least one son, whose name was Thomas, and whose wife's name was Susanna. It seems further, that this Thomas and Susanna Thatcher had at least two sons, viz.: Thomas and Elisha, and four daughters, viz.: Sarah, Susanna, Clorinda, and a fourth whose name we have not learned.

Of this Thomas Thatcher Jr. and his family, we have learned nothing further than the following tombstone inscriptions: "Sacred to the memory of Thomas Thatcher, son of Thomas and Susanna Thatcher, who departed this life April 13th, 1830, in the 77th year of his age." "Sacred to the memory of Aner Thatcher, wife of Thomas Thatcher, who departed this life August, 1845, in the 87th year of her age."

Sarah married Garrett Howell, we believe, who resided near the Delaware Water Gap. They emigrated to Canada in the year 1801, where their numerous descendants now reside. They with a number of other families from New Jersey, settled in the county of Wentworth, and one of the villages of the county is on that account called Jerseyville.

Susanna, as we have seen, became the second wife of John Rosbrugh, nephew of the Clerical Martyr of the Revolution.

Clorinda died single, and the following is her tombstone inscription, viz.: "In memory of Clorinda Thatcher, who departed this life January 28th, A. D. 1826, in the 67th year of her age."

> "Vain world, farewell to you,
>   Heaven is my native air;
> I bid my friends a short adieu,
>   In hopes to meet them there.
>
> I feel my soul released
>   From her old fleshly clod,
> Bright guardian, bear me up in haste
>   And place me near my God."

We see a namesake of her in the person of the oldest daughter of her sister Susanna Thatcher Rosbrugh.

The fourth daughter married Andrew Kitchen, we believe, but we have learned nothing definite of the family.

Elisha married, Oct. 25th, 1796, Mary Coleman, who was born Feb. 1765. The following are the inscriptions on their tombstones. "Sacred to the memory of Elisha Thatcher, who was born Feb. 23d, 1769, and departed this life Nov. 13th, 1845; aged 76 years, 8 months and 20 days."

> "The hour of my departure's come,
>   I hear the voice that calls me home;
> At last O! Lord, let trouble cease,
>   And let thy servant die in peace."

"In memory of Mary Thatcher, wife of Elisha Thatcher, who departed this life April 28th, 1843, in the 79th year of her age."

> My friends, I bid you all farewell,
>   I cannot longer with you dwell,
> My God from pain hath set me free,
>   Prepare for death and follow me."

The children of Elisha and Mary Coleman Thatcher were Samuel, born Oct. 20th 1801, deceased, as the following tombstone inscription indicates: "In memory of Samuel, son of Elisha and Mary Thatcher, who died Sep. 19th, 1802, aged 11 months."

Aaron, deceased, as the following inscription indicates: "In memory of Aaron, son of Elisha and Mary Thatcher, born March 16th, 1810."

Susanna, deceased, as shown by the following inscription: "Susanna, daughter of Elisha and Mary Thatcher, who departed this life Aug. 23d, 1820, aged 12 years, 4 mo's, and 13 days."

> "My kindred friends, weep not for me
>   When in this yard my grave you see,
> My days were few but Christ was he
>   That called me to eternity."

Thomas, born May 26th, 1797, who married Elizabeth Lantz, Nov. 22d, 1822—both deceased.

Mary, who married Jacob Vliet, Oct., 1820—both deceased.

John, born Jan. 19th, 1799, who married Almira ———— and removed to Ohio.

The children of Thomas and Elizabeth Lantz Thatcher, were George L., who married Emily Adaline Boss, March 25th, 1857, and who resides on the south side of the Pohatcong valley, about two miles west of the old Thatcher homestead.

Catharine, who is single, residing in Bloomsbury, Hunterdon county, N. J.

Mary Ann, deceased. Her tombstone inscription is as follows: "In memory of Mary Ann, daughter of Thomas and Elizabeth Thatcher, who died Feb. 19th, 1830, aged 18 d's."

    "An infant to its parents dear,
      Beneath this silent tomb lies here,
    Its spirit is with Christ above,
      To dwell in endless seas of love."

The children of Jacob and Mary Thatcher Vliet were Susanna, Chettie, Mary, Lydia, Garrett, Elisha, David, John, William and Abram. This family resides at Bloomsbury, N. J. One of the daughters married Mr. Adam Warne, who now owns and lives on the original Thatcher homestead.

The children of John A. and Almira Thatcher were, Elisha, who is married, has a family, and resides on the southern slope of the range of hills which separate the Pohatcong and Musconetcong valleys, about three miles east of Bloomsbury, N. J. He has in his possession the old Bible containing the family record of his grand-father, Elisha. The Bible which is supposed to have contained the family record of the Thatchers previous to the generation to which Elisha belonged, was in his possession also until within a few years, but is now believed to be destroyed, nothing being left but a few pictures which were in it.

Elizabeth, born Sep. 23d, 1822, who married William Tonnner; and Aseneth, who married John Fishbaugh, both of whom reside at Hackettstown, Warren county, N. J. Abram, who married Catharine ————, who resides at Belle Vernon; Alfred, who married Drucilla————, residing at Upper Sandusky; Mary, born July 25th, 1824, who married Mr. Rummell; Thomas, deceased, who married Miss Gibson, residing at Tymochtee—all in Wyandot county, Ohio; Amanda, who married Robert Gibson, cousin to Thomas's wife; Samuel, who died single; John, deceased, as the following inscription shows, "In memory of John, son of John A. and Almira Thatcher, who died May 3d, 1844, aged 11 days."; Susanna, deceased, as the following inscription shows, "In memory of Susanna, daughter of John A. and Almira Thatcher, who departed this life Nov 11th, A. D. 1821, aged 2 months and 6 days.", and Sarah, deceased, as the following inscription shows, "In memory of Sarah, daughter of John A. and Almira Thatcher, who died May 11th, A. D. 1840, aged 2 years and 5 days."

B

The following appeared in the *Bethlehem Times*, Bethlehem, Pa., under the date indicated.

"A RELIC OF NORTHAMPTON COUNTY. WEAVERSVILLE, Jan. 1. 1877.

"EDITORS DAILY TIMES: Following is a copy of a receipt in my possession, original in the handwriting of Rev. John Rosbrugh:

'March the fourth one thousand seven hundred and seventy-six, settled with the Reverend Mr. John Rosbrugh Minister of Allen Township Congregation for one year from the first day of May 1775, which I have Rec'd in full of my Steeping (stipend) from said

Congregation, and there is in my hand this day 15£ 19s. 5¼d, as witness my hand this day and date above.   (Signed)   JOHN ROSBRUGH.'

* * "The following circumstances relative to the death of Rev. Mr. Rosbrugh, who was killed at Trenton on the evening of the 2d of January, 1777, are given in the affidavit of Rev. George Duffield, taken from the *Pennsylvania Evening Post* of April 29., 1777: 'As a party of Hessian Yagers marched down the back of the town after the Americans had retreated, they fell in with him, when he surrendered himself a prisoner; notwithstanding which one of them struck him on the head with a sword or cutlass and then stabbed him several times with a bayonet, whilst he implored mercy and begged his life at their hands. This account was given by a Hessian who said that he had killed him (save only that he did not know Mr. Rosbrugh's name, but called him a d——d rebel minister) and that Cour.land Skinner and several other officers, who were present at the relation of the fact, highly applauded the perpetrator for what he had done. After he was massacred he was stripped naked, and in that condition left lying in an open field, till taken up and buried near the place by some of the inhabitants.'

"His widow afterwards received a pension from the Government. We find that the Supreme Executive Council of Pennsylvania, in pursuance of an act passed March 27th, 1790, caused an order to be drawn upon the Treasurer in favor of Mrs. Jane Rosbrugh, widow of Rev. John Rosbrugh, for the sum of 204£ 15s, being the amount of pension due to her from the 18th of May, 1788, until the 18th of May, 1790, according to the Comptroller General's Reports and an Order of the Orphans' Court of Northampton Co."

C

ROBERT ROSBRUGH FAMILY. We have obtained the following information relative to the family of Robert Rosbrugh, nephew of the Clerical Martyr of the Revolution, who removed south in 1783. He had at least one son, named Hilkiah, who lived in Ohio, but died in Va., when about 40 years of age, leaving a son, Robert, in Va., and 5 or 7 other sons in Ohio—e. g. Henry Rosebrugh, Loganville, Logan Co., O.—whilst some may be found in Indiana. Robert died in Bedford Co., Va., Nov. 1st, 1877, in a good old age, an elder in the Presbyterian church, respected by all. He left four daughters—all married—the youngest of whom is the wife of Rev. John Ruff, pastor of the Presbyterian church of Buford, Bedford Co., Va. The pastor of the Mossy Creek Presbyterian church, Augusta Co., Va., is also a descendant, we believe, of Robert Rosbrugh who went to North Carolina in 1783.

ADDENDA.

The following additional items of information relative to the descendants of the Clerical Martyr of the Revolution, came to hand too late for insertion in their proper place. They have been furnished by Mr. James Rosebrugh, Amboy, Lee county, Illinois.

2d Generation. *James*, it seems, was married October 18th, instead of 12th, 1792.

3d Generation. *Jane* (Leaming) died March 12th 1833. *John* died October 9th, 1874. His wife, Mary Goheen (not Gohene), was the daughter of Edward and Christiana Goheen. She was born July 29th, 1800, married September 8th, instead of 7th, 1818, and died May 22d, 1880. *Hugh Wilson* died May 17th, 1802. *James Ralston* is dead but the date of his decease we have not learned. He had four children, all of whom are dead. His only surviving descendant is a little grand-son, who resides with his mother in Groveland, Livingston county, New York. The family record, we believe, is in the possession of Mr. George Kelly, brother of Mr. Rosebrugh's wife. His wife, Christiana Kelly, was the daughter of Major Daniel and Mary Kelly. *Ezra* died February 2d, 1877. *Margaret* (Baldwin) died October 11th, 1840.

4th Generation. *Miranda* (not Amanda), daughter of John and Mary Goheen, was born March 16th instead of 6th, 1800, married Bazaleel Alvord, born June 4th, 1814, son of Chester and Susan Alvord, July 27th, 1837, and died March 16th, 1838. *James* married, November 8th, 1849, Sarah Lucretia Bottom, born January 12th, 1822, daughter of David and Lucretia Bottom. *Anna Maria* married, October 30th, 1854, John Wesley Norris, born July 23d, 1828. He died July 12th, 1852. She married, April 2d, 1862, Clinton A. Blackmer, son of Cherles and Eleanor Blackmer. *John Ralston*, a son whose name we had not learned, born January 5th, 1829, married, November 9th, 1852, Julia E., born February 14th, 1832, daughter of Ashel and Elizabeth Taylor. *Charles Wilson* died at Camden, South Carolina, February 27th, 1865, while with Sherman on his march upon Richmond. He entered the service in the 13th Illinois volunteers, served his three years and reenlisted for the war. *Margaret Baldwin* married, December 25th, 1867, Alonzo Dee, born April 13th, 1835, son of Alonzo and Asenith Hosmer. *Patience Elizabeth* married, December 25th, 1867, Sylvester Perry (not P. C.) Hosmer, brother of Margaret's husband, and who was born October 11th, 1842.

5th Generation. The children of James and Lucretia Bottom Rosebrugh of the 4th generation were, *Theron Alexis*, born August 12th, 1851. *Kate Adel*, born September 18th, 1853, married, December 24th, 1879, Frederic Lyman Geddes born November 10th, 1850, son of Norman and Laura Casey Geddes. *James C. Clark*, born May 8th, 1857. The son of John Ralston and Julia Taylor Rosebrugh of the 4th generation, is *Harry Pierpont*, born July 31st, 1853. The daughter of Alonzo Dee and Margaret Baldwin Rosebrugh Hosmer of the 4th generation, is *Mary Rosebrugh*, born September 19th, 1868. The children of Sylvester P. and Patience Elizabeth Rosebrugh Hosmer of the 4th generation, are *Asenith Beddlecome*, born December 9th, 1868, and *John Rosebrugh*, born January 28th, 1872.

www.ingramcontent.com/pod-product-compliance
Lightning Source LLC
Chambersburg PA
CBHW020145170426
43199CB00010B/898